About the Author

Karl Bradshaw-White was born in London in 1962, educated at Tylney Hall Boarding school in Hampshire. He has been an antiques and fine arts dealer and has worked in furniture restoration for 30 years. He is a self-taught artist exhibited at Beecroft art gallery in Southend, picking up a Beecroft award for work displayed.

He entered the world of miniature making in the late 1990's becoming one of the only artists in the world to specialise in Pietra Dura, a 17th century art working in marble and semi-precious stones, with work displayed in museums around the world. Karl is now semi-retired living with his partner of 35 years.

Dedication

Dedicated to my partner and travel companion of 35 years.

Karl Bradshaw-White

ALGARVE TRAVEL GUIDE

54 Cities/Towns/Villages

AUSTIN MACAULEY
PUBLISHERS LTD.

A CIP catalogue record for this title is available from the British Library.

ISBN 978 1 78455 259 6

www.austinmacauley.com

First Published (2015)
Austin Macauley Publishers Ltd.
25 Canada Square
Canary Wharf
London
E14 5LB

Printed and bound in Great Britain

Acknowledgments

My thanks to Hayley Knight, Senior Editor of Austin Macauley, for a chance meeting, and giving me the encouragement to write this book.

Contents

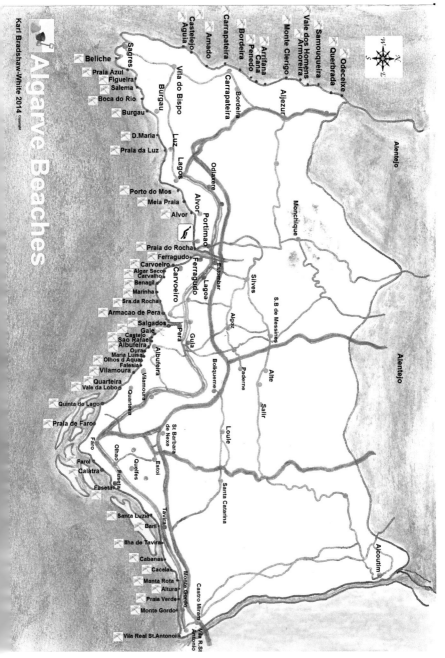

Algarve Beaches

Karl Bradshaw-White 2014

13

A Brief History of the Algarve

Portugal has a long history which could easily fill the whole book; here we give you a brief insight into the Algarve. The Algarve has been found to go back to Stone Age; evidence can still be seen today, in the form of megalithic stones (called menhirs) found in Vila do Bispo. Jumping past other ancient periods to the Romans, we find settlements in the Algarve as early as the 2nd century BC: as with many countries, the rivers and the coast were always important to control. Much evidence of Roman settlements has been discovered in the Algarve. One fine example well worth a visit is in the centre of Vilamoura: a preserved Roman site and museum, Cerro da Vila. Other sites include Lagos, Estoi, and Praia do Luz.

By the 5th century AD the Roman occupation had ceased; the Algarve was now in control by Visigoths who had defeated many Roman armies. Their rule was to last until 711, a year which saw the arrival of the Moors, who swiftly conquered much of the Algarve including the important towns of Lagos and Silves. They settled, establishing themselves like no others had done before. Soon the whole region was under their rule. By 716 they named it Al-Gharb meaning 'The West'. The Moors ruled for more than 500 years, until 1249. In a long takeover bid during the Reconquista, the Kingdom of Portugal conquered the region in a series of successful military campaigns against the Moors that lasted years.

Not wanting to give up what they had ruled for more than 500 years, Islamic armies tried to regain what they had lost. From 1242 a new Kingdom of the Algarve was formed, and by 1250 the Algarve was fully controlled by Portugal. The main capital of Portugal shifted to Lisbon in 1255. Portugal continued to push the Moors back, even conquering parts of North Africa which were now they classed as part of the Algarve. In the 13th century Portugal and England became great allies; this led to Portugal being able to grow in size. By the fifteenth and sixteenth centuries Portugal ranked in size, stature and importance with England and Spain. The Algarve was now well established, having great farming potential and as a trading post with ships leaving for other continents trading spices and slaves, with Lagos as the capital. Then everything crumbled when the earthquake of 1755 destroyed most of Portugal and the Algarve. It still is one of the worst earthquakes ever reported causing so much destruction and thought to have been a 9 on the Richter scale. The fact that it fell on November the first, the public holiday of All Saints' Day, meant that the death toll was one of the worst in history.

In later years the Algarve carried on defending itself from others who tried to conquer it and failed. The best known was the Peninsular War which lasted seven years at the start of the 19th century before Napoleon was defeated and captured. The Algarve saw its own King and Governor until the formation of the Portuguese republic in 1910, when the Kingdom of the Algarve disappeared. Portugal then saw another war in 1961, known as the Colonial War: Portugal fought against her African colonies, including those of the Algarve in Northern Africa. The dictatorship of Salazar ended in 1974, overthrown by a military coup. Now a public holiday is celebrated on April 25th each year, known across Portugal as Freedom day.

A to Z travel Tips

Airports

Contact information for Major UK Airports

Aberdeen Tel: 0844 481 6666
www.aberdeenairport.com

Belfast International Tel: 028 9448 4848
www.belfastairport.com

Birmingham Tel: 0844 567 6000
www.birminghamairport.co.uk

Bristol Tel: 0871 334 4444
www.bristolairport.co.uk

Cardiff Tel: 01446 711 111
www.tbicardiffairport.com

East Midlands Tel: 0871 919 9000
www.eastmidlandsairport.com

Edinburgh Tel: 0844 481 8989
www.edinburghairport.com

Glasgow Tel: 0844 481 5555
www.glasgowairport.com

Glasgow Preswick Tel: 0871 223 0700
www.glasgowpreswick.com

Leeds Bradford Tel: 0871 288 2288
www.leedsbradfordairport.com

Liverpool John Lennon Tel: 0871 521 8484
www.liverpoolairport.com

London Gatwick Tel: 0844 892 0322
www.gatwickairport.com

London Heathrow Tel: 0844 335 1801
www.heathrowairport.com

London Luton Tel: 01582 405 100
www.london-luton.co.uk

London Stansted Tel: 0844 335 0711
www.stanstedairport.com

Manchester Tel: 0871 271 0711
www.manchesterairport.com

Newcastle Tel:0871 882 1121
www.newcastleairport.com

Contact information for Portugal Airports

Acores Tel: 351 29 6205400
www.ana.pt

Beja Tel: 351 284 001 020
www.ana.pt

Faro Tel: 351 289 800 800
www.ana.pt

Lisbon Tel: 351 21 8413500
www.ana.pt

Porto Tel: 351 22 9432400
www.ana.pt

Airport Transfers & Taxis

In this section we explain the difference between airport transfer companies and that of the traditional taxi.

Whilst both taxis and transfer companies must both be licensed and insured to carry passengers, the taxi can be hailed at any point. They will have a light on the roof showing if they are already carrying passengers, or free to pick up passengers. They must carry a meter that will show the minimum fare on the meter. As of 2014 the daytime minimum rate is €3.45. This rate runs during the hours of 6:30am to 9:00pm. The rate then changes to a minimum of €4.10, as the night-time period is considered as unsociable working hours. Unless you have already used a licensed taxi to your current destination in the past, you are unlikely to know the cost of the journey. The driver normally holds a distance chart that will give you a rough guide to the cost of your journey. Often there can be a language problem; we suggest that you write on a piece of paper the phrase, 'Quanto irá custar o meu destino?' (How much will my destination cost?).

Airport transfers, known as transfer companies, can take you to many destinations other than just the airport. These will need to be booked in advance as they are only fully licensed to take you to pre-booked destinations and may not be flagged down or hailed. The price is given in advance and you must either pre-pay for your journey online in advance or when you reach your destination. Never pay up front in cash as this is against the law and licensed transfer companies will not ask for it.

If booking a return journey to the airport, then normal practice to pay for the return when you reach your destination, as after all you have pre-booked.

The advantage to using an airport transfer company is that you know they will be there to greet you at the airport terminal, rather than taking a chance of getting a taxi, as you could be left waiting.

You will also find that most airport transfer companies use minibuses or people-carriers, with the advantage of carrying larger groups along with plenty of luggage space. Nowadays they even have Wi-Fi on board which gives you the advantage of booking in for your flight whilst on the way to the airport.

Entrance to Faro Airport

Bike Hire

Most hotels will give information on local companies. There are also companies, listed below, that will deliver to your resort or villa for a small delivery charge.

A good reputable one will also offer cycle helmets (recommended) and other forms of body padding. If you are looking for more of an adventure, a weekly activity group meets in the Algarve. They can be contacted on: www.activityalgarve.com

For those looking for specialised biking holidays then see www.algarvebikeholidays.com

Bike shops

www.bikeland.pt Tel: 289358379
Email:bikelandshop@gmail.com

Cascalheira EN125 Quatro Estrades, Quarteira, Algarve 8125-018

www.bikesul.pt Tel: 282 339 636
Email:geral@bikesul.pt

Rua Candido dos Reis, Nº62 S B Messines 8375-105, Algarve.

Budgeting your holiday

Budgeting whilst on holiday need not be about *what* you spend but more about *how* you spend.

Accommodation

If booking a hotel ask if they have any all-inclusive deals like half board or full board: it may be something you have not considered. Sometimes the extra cost can work out a lot cheaper in the long run. If you are booking self-catering or private villas look on the availability calendar. Often there can be an eight to nine day gap available, and the owners would sooner have it fully booked rather having than one to three days that are dead dates.

Car hire

Try to speak to the company by telephone rather than email, as what you will save in a deal will outweigh the cost of a phone call. Tell them you are looking at different companies for the best deal. Choose a basic model; ask if they would offer you an upgrade to a larger car, or one with air conditioning. If they offer toll pre-payment (around €20), ask if they can include it in the deal. Once they agree, give them your email address and ask them to confirm the deal, allowing you to check with other companies for a better deal before committing yourself.

Dining out

Many restaurants offer dish of the day (Prato do Dia) at lunchtimes, priced at €6-10. This will include bread, olives, main meal, wine or beer, desert, coffee. For evening meals many restaurants offer a choice from a set menu. Prices range from €12-15: they would cost around €20 if ordered from the main menu.

Ask for the set menu first as it will not be offered automatically. If choosing from the main menus ask about the cover (couvert): this is the basket of bread, butter, olives, and sardine paté. Some restaurants charge per person rather than per portion: often a table of four people will get the same portion as one person, but charged four times! This is not done to cheat you, as each restaurant has its own policy.

Shopping

Only in the past ten years have supermarkets in Portugal succumbed to convenience foods. It is easy to put things in a supermarket trolley like ready-washed lettuce in a bag, but you will pay ten times the price of a good homegrown lettuce from your local daily market. Most towns and villages will have a daily indoor market selling fresh fish and produce every day. Don't worry that you do not speak the language, as choosing what you want is usually self-help; the traders then weigh what you have chosen. You would also be missing out on the real Portugal. Fish might be a little more expensive, but it will be a fresh catch that morning from the Atlantic Ocean, rather than farm-reared from another country.

Car Hire

Most people will pre-book their car before arrival; most will use a well-known company. Many people look for that bargain deal; these are a few tips to check.

Does the insurance cover include accidental waver? Normally just third party insurance is offered. If full insurance is not offered there will be an added extra charge when picking up the car: this can be from €300-€1000. Think about getting a stand-alone policy before you travel. Websites like www.travelsupermarkets.com have comparison prices. Child seats are often offered free of charge. Do they offer a pre-payment method for motorway tolls? This can be a one-off fee of around €20.00. If no toll pre-payment is offered, make sure when you pay at a post office that it includes *your* use and not the last user of the car. Check that it covers a named driver, as should you be unable to drive then you need a named driver on the insurance. Are you covered should you take a trip across to Spain?

When booking and picking up the car from the airport, give an address you will be staying at. Take your time to check the car for any signs of damage, and make sure it is noted on the form. Check the tyres, as if stopped by police you, as the driver, are responsible. Check the hire vehicle has a fluorescent jacket, and a warning triangle: these are compulsory to carry by law. Ask what the fuel arrangement is: normally it is picked up with a full tank and returned with a full tank. Ask for a free map: most companies will have them.

Campsites

See full listing in index.

Clock changes

Portugal has the same time change as the UK. Listed below are the estimated clock changes for the next five years.

Year	Clocks go forward 1hr	Clocks go back 1hr
2015	Sunday 29 March, 01:00	Sunday 25 October, 02:00

2016	Sunday 27 March, 01:00	Sunday 30 October, 02:00
2017	Sunday 26 March, 01:00	Sunday 29 October, 02:00
2018	Sunday 25 March, 01:00	Sunday 28 October, 02:00
2019	Sunday 31 March, 01:00	Sunday 27 October, 02:00

Clothing

Even during the summer months it is worthwhile packing a lightweight sweater or jacket as the cool evenings can feel nippy, especially near the coast and also if travelling inland to places like Monchique mountain. If entering public buildings including shops, markets and supermarkets, it is frowned upon to enter wearing only a bathing suit or shorts; you may well be asked to leave.

Clothes & Shoe sizes

Ladies' clothes sizes

| UK | 8 | 10 | 12 | 14 | 16 | 18 | 20 | 22 |
| EU | 36 | 38 | 40 | 42 | 44 | 46 | 48 | 50 |

Men's clothes sizes

| UK | 36 | 38 | 40 | 42 | 44 | 46 | 48 |
| EU | 46 | 48 | 50 | 52 | 54 | 56 | 58 |

Children's clothes sizes

| Height (cm) | 56 | 62 | 68 | 74 | 80 | 86 |
| Age Months | 0-3 | 3-6 | 6-9 | 9-12 | 12-18 | 18-24 |

| Height (cm) | 92 | 98 | 104 | 110 | 116 | 122 | 128 | 134 | 140 |
| Age (years) | 2-3 | 3-4 | 4-5 | 5-6 | 6-7 | 7-8 | 8 9 | 9-10 | 11-12 |

Adult shoe sizes

| UK | 2 | 3 | 4 | 5 | 6 | 7 | 8 | 9 | 10 | 11 | 12 |
| EU | 34 | 37 | 38 | 39 | 40 | 41 | 42 | 43 | 44 | 45 | 46 |

Children's shoe sizes

UK	0	1	2	3	4	5	6	7	8	9	10
EU	16	17	18	19	20	21	22	23	25	27	28

Computers

Portugal has now installed many Wi-Fi areas in shopping centres along beach fronts and in popular tourist areas near the tourist information centres, and this Wi-Fi is free. But remember, you must have your wireless security switched on or others can log themselves onto your laptop, even via mobile phone, and steal your information.

Tip: On the back of your laptop to will see a little hole with a padlock sign. This is for a Kensington lock, a steel cable which allows you to lock your laptop to a solidly fixed item, so there is no need to carry it around when not in use. The cables cost around £5-10 and can be purchased from most electrical retail outlets.

Crime

Crime figures have dropped in the Algarve in the last few years. There used to be reports of personal attacks on tourists, mainly in the Albufeira area. These all occurred in the late evening and early hours of the morning. Now with a greater police presence during holiday season these crimes have all but disappeared. Petty crime still remains as it does across most of Europe; things to watch for are pickpockets at busy markets and opportunist crimes with people not being aware when putting down handbags and mobile devices at busy bars and restaurants. Other petty crime involves car break-ins on rental cars when left at beach car parks and well-known tourist beauty spots.

Car hire companies are now making it less obvious that the cars are rentals by removing car hire advertising from their vehicles. Should you be the victim of a crime you must report it at a police station within 24 hours. Obtain a crime report for you to make a claim on insurance; this report costs around

€10.00, and a receipt is given to claim the fee back when submitting a claim.

Currency

Portugal is one the many European Union countries whose common official currency is the euro.

One euro is divided into 100 cents. The coins come in denominations of 1, 2, 5, 10, 20 and 50 cents, and 1 and 2 euros.

The notes are differentiated by their size and colour and come in denominations of 5, 10, 20, 50, 100, 200 and 500 euros. However since 2010 the 500 note has been used less in circulation due to money laundering.

Custom/Currency allowance

Most people will have their 'holiday head' on and not realise there are restrictions for entering Portugal. Below are the guidelines for August 2014. Remember these are for personal use per person.

Arriving with goods purchased within the EU: Tobacco, 800 Cigarettes, 400 cigarillos (max. 3g each), 200 cigars, or 1kg Pipe or rolling tobacco (you must be 17 years or older). Alcohol, 10 litres of spirits over 22%, 20 litres of alcoholic drinks of less than 22%, 90 litres of wine (though no more than 60 litres of sparkling wine), 110 litres of beer.

Free import to passengers arriving from non-EU member states (including Aland Island, Canary Islands, Channel Islands and other similar territories): Tobacco, Beers and Spirits (you must be at least 17 years of age) 200 cigarettes; or 100 cigarillos (max 3g each); or 50 cigars; or 250g of tobacco litre of spirits over 22% volume, or non-denatured ethyl alcohol with more than 80% volume; or 2 litres of spirits or aperitifs made of wine or similar less than 22% volume, or sparkling wines or liqueur wines, 4 litres of wine or 16 litres of beer.

Medicine products: sufficient for your journey and for personal use only.

Other goods for air travellers up to a total value of €430 (adults), or €150 per passenger aged less than 15 years.

Currency Import regulations: import of local currency (Euro-EUR) and foreign currencies are without restrictions.

If you are entering the country with more than €5,000 it is a good idea to declare it upon arrival as you could find delays if you return with more than €5,000.

Disabled information

Help/Aid at Airports

On arrival you will find help as soon as you get off the plane, from assistance getting to the passport control to organising collection of luggage which can be arranged free of charge. At the airport disabled passengers are boarded onto planes before other passengers. At the aircraft door, you will need to transfer onto a narrower aisle-chair so the assistants can get you to your seat – therefore an aisle seat is often dedicated to disabled passengers. All the major airports in Portugal have disabled toilets as well as lifts and ramps. There are many companies that offer airport transfer with wheelchair access as well as some car hire companies that offer adapted vehicles: Euro Cars, to name just one. If you need to hire wheelchairs or electric (battery operated) mobility scooters then Portugal has different companies that offer them for hire.

Disabled Parking in Portugal

Most shops will have dedicated places for disabled drivers; some car parks allow vehicles displaying a disabled parking sign to park free of charge.

There are no concessions for disabled drivers on roadside parking, unless you use the dedicated parking spaces. Each town and village will have one.

Do not park in a disabled spot if the sign has letters and numbers, as this will be a dedicated parking spot for that vehicle. Portugal along with the rest of Europe operates the blue badge system, but the police are tolerant of just a disabled sign or sticker as long as the driver has a genuine disability.

One of many hire companies in Portugal

Public Transport

All public transport used on urban routes has four seats reserved for people with walking difficulties. Most have no access for the users of wheelchairs; most drivers will help you on, unless your movement is completely restricted. The blind may travel with guide dogs if they are on a leash and wear a muzzle. They can also travel with their dogs at no extra cost. Some rent-a-car companies have automatic and specially adapted vehicles available for hire.

Radio

The following radio stations are broadcast in English and list news weather, and events:

www.kissfm.pt/ broadcast on102.1fm

www.magicfmalgarve.com/ broadcast on 98.00fm

Rail Travel

Rail travel in Portugal in general can be a bit of a let-down for those who are wheelchair-bound or need to use a mobility scooter. Most trains do not accommodate those with mobility needs. However Portugal does have one such train, the Alpha Pendular. This train is fitted with a platform hoist for wheelchairs. It has a carriage solely dedicated for the disabled with a large wheelchair painted on the side of the carriage, so easy to find. The carriage has wheelchair-friendly toilets, with a large sliding door. The train runs from Tunes in the Central Algarve straight to Lisbon.

Driving

Vehicles drive on the right in Portugal, as does most of Europe; vehicles coming from the right have priority and at intersections.

You will find that since the year 2005 the Algarve has seen many new roundabouts spring up. They may not appear on most satellite navigation systems. Vehicles already on the roundabout have right of way. When entering a motorway you must slow down or stop: you do not have the right to pull straight out.

Road signs comply with international rules. Compulsory papers you must carry: Driving licence, Motor insurance certificate, Vehicle registration, or equivalent.

Speed limits

20 kph – in built-up areas
50-70 kph – normal roads when indicated
90 kph – on normal roads
100 kph – on roads restricted to motor vehicles
120 kph – on motorways.

It is illegal to drive with a blood alcohol level of 0.5 grams per litre or more. On-the-spot fines are issued, with receipts always given. All occupants must wear seat belts. You must stop at zebra crossings in Portugal. Use of mobile phones whilst driving is forbidden, unless using hands-free equipment such as Bluetooth. As of 2014 it is now illegal to use double ear plug earphone for phones and all listening devices.

You will find road rage does not exist in most of Portugal, but a lack of indicators is common so patience is a must. Do not use your horn in such situations.

One common mistake most people make whilst on holiday is the crossing of single or double white lines. When using a roundabout you may only use the outside lane if taking the first exit. If taking the second, third or fourth exits you must use the inside lane; failure can incur a fine from €60-€300.

Parking

The first rule for parking is to remember that it is an offence to park facing the wrong way: you must park the same flow as the traffic on that side of the road. Car parks are also seen as public places so driving without a seat belt being worn is a fineable offence.

In cities you will find pay and display areas known as Blue Zones. Failure to pay and display will lead to your car being towed away. Road signs are standard as throughout Europe.

Accidents and Breakdowns

All hire cars come with breakdown cover as standard; should you break down you must wear the fluorescent jacket that is compulsory to carry in the car, as well as the warning triangle.

In the event of a breakdown safely place the warning triangle at the rear of the vehicle at a distance of 25 metres; breakdown cover will also cover punctures.

In the event of an accident you must leave the vehicle where the accident happened. Do not attempt to move the vehicle or pull over to the side, as police attendance is normal for all accidents, no matter how minor. They will measure the accident scene and give a police report. The same applies for wearing the fluorescent jacket and placing the warning triangle. For accidents call police Tel: 112.

Electricity

Electric current is 220V, frequency 50 Hertz; current sockets accord with European standards. Blade plugs require a transformer for 220 volts and adapter plug. Plugs on appliances in Portugal do not require fuses.

Embassies and Consulates

AUSTRALIA

Av.da liberdade 200, Lisbon
Tel:(+351) 213 101 500

BRITISH

Lisbon – British Embassy
Address Rua de São Bernardo 33
1249-082 Lisbon
Phone: (+351) 392.4000
Lisbon – British Consulate
Address Rua de São Bernardo No 33
1249-082 Lisbon
Phone: (+351) 392.4159

Portimão – British Consulate
Address Apartado 609
Edificio A Fabrica
Avenida Guanaré
8501-915 Portimao

Phone: (+351) 282 490.750

CANADA

Embassy of Canada in Lisbon,
Avenida da Liberdade,
Nr. 196-200, 3rd Floor ,
1269-121 Lisbon, Portugal
Phone: (011 351) 21 316 46 00
Fax: (011 351) 21 316 46 93
Email: lsbon-cs@international.gc.ca

Consulate of Canada in Faro,
Rua Frei Lourenco de Santa Maria No.1,
1st Floor, Partado 79
8001 Faro, Portugal
Phone: (011 351) 289 80 37 57
Fax: (011 351) 289 88 08 88
Email: consul.faro.canada@net.novis.pt

EIRE

Embassy of Ireland in Portugal Rua da Imprensa a Estrela 1-4
1200-684 Lisbon
Phone: +351-21-392-9440
Fax: +351-21-397-7363
Email: Lisbonembassy@dfa.ie

Emergencies

The national emergency telephone number for Police, Ambulance, and Fire is 112. If you need non-emergency medical attention most towns will have a Centro de Saúde.

You can produce your EHIC blue health card for the UK (formerly E111), or your European health card for your country within the EU.

Gay and Lesbian

Many might think that Portugal, being a prominent Roman Catholic country at nearly 80%, would not tolerate homosexuality. In May 2010 it became the eighth country in the world to allow same sex marriage. It even allows for a partner to take the other's surname in the marriage ceremony. There are many gay clubs throughout the Algarve, as well as accommodation. Showing affection in public is common with the holding of hands, but passionate kissing in public is rarely seen.

Language

Portuguese is the official language of more than 250 million people worldwide, the largest number being in Brazil. Brazilian Portuguese has always been slightly different in spelling, but in 2009 it was agreed that Brazil would adopt the new spellings now standardised.

As part of this new standardisation, silent consonants have been removed in order for words to be spelt more phonetically: for example "optimo" (great) into "otimo". New changes should waive the need for various accents, but this may not be the case for what is sometimes known as Algarvian, as Portuguese spoken in the Algarve is often spoken faster than that spoken in Lisbon. It is often classed as almost slang.

Learning the language can be easy for those who studied Latin. As often in Latin it is the object that comes first. A simple example is "pão fatiado" (literally, 'bread sliced'). You will also notice there is little use of the letters K, W and Y in words. These letters have now been added to the Portuguese alphabet.

Mobile phones

Portugal has very good signal strength even in the most remote of places.

Lost or stolen mobile phone

To find your IMEI number, enter: * # 0 6 # (star hash zero six hash) on the keypad. This number is something all mobile phones will have. If a mobile is lost or stolen, call your provider give them the IMEI number. They will suspend the service and the phone may be traced (depending on network). If the theft is to be reported, supply the police with the IMEI number. Your phone provider will be able to give you a replacement sim card. Provided you report it as soon as possible your credit (assuming you are on a pay as you go tariff) will be credited to your new sim card. Your provider will not be able to supply you with contact numbers that were stored on your phone or sim card. However, you can ask for your phone call history, giving you numbers dialled on your phone.

Note: It is important that you do not store your credit/debit card pin numbers on your mobile device. If you have to store them on your phone give them another name that you can easily remember. Do not give them names like (Barclays or Visa). Also, add a prefix number like 0044, as if your phone is stolen along with your wallet or purse, a thief will go through your phone looking for four-digit numbers. A four-digit number will easily tell them it could be a card pin number. Before you give up on your lost phone try calling it: check at a local police station to see if it has been handed in.

Money Matters

ATMs – Automatic Teller Machines (Multibanco)

Portugal has a national network of cash machines (ATMs) identified by the symbol MB (Multibanco), from which you can withdraw cash 24 hours a day.

It is unfortunate to say that whilst on holiday wallets/purses are lost or stolen all over the world and not just Portugal. When traveling abroad it is a good idea to empty wallets and purses to a minimum, as many cards you carry will never be used whilst on holiday. This will save you the trouble of having to report them in any such event – the same way that it is not wise to carry large amounts of money. Due to the chip and pin system being introduced, it is common when wallets/purses are stolen that they are nearly always found with all the contents except the cash, as the cards are of no use without the pin. Do check at your nearest police station as quite often they are handed in: the Portuguese are honest people.

Multibank Symbol

Mosquito Bites & Insect Stings

Avoiding mosquito bites

The mosquito (from the Portuguese word for little fly) is a common insect in Portugal and the Algarve and known as the gnat. Below we give you information about the insect, for now let us cover what you need to know. There is no risk of malaria in Portugal. However, it was reported that the island of Madeira has had cases of dengue fever as late as 2012. This is very rare but it can be life-threatening if it turns into dengue haemorrhagic fever.

It has also been known in very hot weather for some larger varieties to come from far afield as North Africa. The bite can be very severe and itchy. Mosquitoes prefer some people over others. This preference about who they bite is down to whose sweat simply smells better than others. This is because of the proportions of carbon dioxide, octenol and other compounds that make up body odour.

It is also known that shower gels and creams can cause attraction: these are ones that contain almond oil and honey extracts. If you normally take a glass of water to bed, then this will also attract mosquitoes; instead take a bottle of water.

Mosquitoes go through four stages in their life-cycle: egg, larva, pupa and adult.

Only the females bite as well as laying their eggs normally in standing water, such as around plants, or an artificial water container such as a plastic bucket.

The first three stages are aquatic and last 5–14 days, depending on the species and the ambient temperature; eggs hatch to become larvae, then pupae and can be seen wriggling in the water. The adult mosquito emerges from the pupa as it floats at the water surface. Adults live for 4–8 weeks.

There is a powerful semiochemical that triggers the mosquito's keen sense of smell; a large part of the mosquito's sense of smell is devoted to sniffing out human targets.

Better to apply a repellent as prevention rather than treating a bite. Mosquitoes produce a chemical while biting: when they place their snout into your skin you cannot feel it. Once they have fed it is this chemical that cause itching. Scratching the bits with your nails will likely lead to an infection, so avoid scratching at all cost. Placing an ice cube will help. There are about 3,500 species of mosquitoes found throughout the world. In some species of mosquito, the females feed on humans, and are therefore vectors for a number of infectious diseases affecting millions of people per year. Mosquitoes have mouthparts that are adapted for piercing the skin of plants and animals. While males typically feed on nectar and plant juices, the female needs to obtain nutrients from a 'blood meal' before she can produce eggs. We hope this description will help you not to be their next victim.

Insect repellents

The chemical DEET repels some mosquitoes and other insects. Repellents recommended by the CDC (the US Center for Disease Control) are Picaridin, Oil of Eucalyptus, Jungle Wipes and Avon SOS (Skin So Soft). If you do not have any repellent to hand, rubbing the oil from the skin of a freshly-picked lemon will help ease the pain. (Try vinegar for wasp and bee stings as the acid is a neutralizer when placed on cotton wool over the sting; only a bee sting will leave behind the sting point from the bee and this needs to be removed with tweezers.)

Wasps

The common wasp in most countries can build a nest that can hold up to 5000 wasps in one nest; however, the more common in Portugal are those that make small nests that hang by a small stem. These nests should be left alone, and little harm will come.

However, if you have to destroy one it is better with the spray type of pesticide. This should only be done early morning and late evening as this is when the wasps are at their most docile. There is also an earth wasp that lives in the ground; this gives a sting that is very painful, often needing medical attention – an anti-histamine injection followed by a course of anti-inflammatory tablets – as it can give a reaction of bad swelling.

Bees

Most of Portugal will have honeybees which are harmless; however, they will sting if provoked. Unlike the wasp that can sting over and over, a bee will only sting the once, leaving behind the sting. It is important to remove this as soon as possible with tweezers as it will continue to pump venom. If swelling gets large in less than five minutes seek medical help as soon as possible.

Scorpions

Portugal has small black scorpions, found under pots and rocks, that can give a nasty but not life-threatening sting. They are normally never seen, and the chance of seeing one on holiday is very slim. If found leave alone and they will return to hide in the darkness which they prefer.

Public Holidays

Fixed holiday dates	_Portuguese name_
January 1st New Year's Day	(Ano Novo)
April 25th Liberty day	(Dia da Liberdade)
May 1st Labour Day	(Dia do Trabahlo)
June 10th Portugal Day	(Dia de Portugal)
August 15th Assumption Day	(Assuncao)
October 5th Republic Day	(Herois da Repuplica)
November 1st All Saint's Day	(Todas os Santos)
December 1st Independence Day	(Dia da Independencia)
December 8th Immaculate Conception	(Imaculada Conceiao)
December 25th Christmas Day	(Natal)

Movable holiday dates	
February Shrove Tuesday	
April Good Friday	(Sexta-feria Santa)
April Easter Sunday	(Pascoa)
May-June Corpus Christi	(Corpo de Dues)

Please note: some public holiday & religious holidays may no longer be classed as a public holiday, even though it will still be celebrated.

Smoking

Portugal came into line with most other European countries on the banning of smoking in enclosed public places; these include shopping centres which may have open spaces where smoking is permitted. Some bars and restaurants will have a smoking room that is completely separated. Fines for breaching this law range from €50-€750.

Weather and Seasons

Spring

Spring is a magical time to visit Portugal and the Algarve, as it starts to come alive with wild flowers starting to bloom. Temperatures reach an average 18 to 20ºC and there is plenty of sunshine. With these mild temperatures, spring is popular with the golfers and walkers, with beach life starting to show signs of summer around the corner. The evenings can feel colder than they actually are, but it is still possible to eat outside in the evenings. (See Clock changes in A-Z information guide.)

Almond blossom in spring

Summer

In the summer months, which have an average of 12 hours of sunshine per day, temperatures tend to be around 30-35ºC; it has been known to reach 40ºC. The Algarve is on the Atlantic coast so gets the gently cooling breeze that Lisbon does not get. It is worth checking the papers for the UV count as this can reach high numbers. Keep villas cool by closing windows and doors as the house are built to stay cool in summer months.

Summer time sees the butterflies out and about

Autumn

As temperatures start to cool to an average of 17-20°C, autumn is an ideal time to visit and explore those places you would find too hot and bothered in the summer months. With the start of the golfers arriving, shorts can still be worn at this time of year. The sun sits lower in the sky during the autumn but still gives nine hours of sunshine to enjoy. Little rain is seen until about November.

Autumn sees many fiery sunsets

Winter

Winter months give up to six hours of sunshine a day, with average temperatures around 16-18ºC. During the end of December to January it is the rainy season and whilst it can rain very heavily most days still give some hours of sun. The evening can dip to as low as 7ºC; you can get some colder, windier days. You can see the almond trees in blossom and the young lambs and kid goats if you are visiting the Algarve in January or February with the start of the Carnival season in Portugal toward the end of February.

Month	Jan	Feb	Mar	Apr	May	Jun	Jul	Aug	Sep	Oct	Nov	Dec
Average Day Temp °C (°F)	16.1 (61)	16.7 (62.1)	18.4 (65.1)	19.8 (67.6)	24.4 (75.9)	25.4 (77.7)	28.7 (83.7)	28.8 (83.8)	26.7 (80.1)	23.1 (73.6)	19.4 (66.9)	16.7 (62.1)
Average Night Temp°C (°F)	7.7 (45.9)	8.4 (47.1)	8.9 (48)	10.4 (50.7)	12.5 (54.5)	15.7 (60.3)	17.9 (64.2)	18.0 (64.4)	16.9 (62.4)	14.3 (57.7)	10.9 (51.6)	8.6 (47.5)
Avg. precipitation days	12	13	9	10	7	4	1	1	3	9	10	11
Sun Hours	170.5	165.2	232.5	252.0	313.1	333.0	368.9	353.4	273.0	226.3	183.0	167.4

Campsites in Algarve

Campsite Turiscampo**** (Western Algarve)

Campsite suitable for handicapped persons
Opening period: 01/01 up to and including 31/12
Price Guide: €28.00–€36.00
Number of touring pitches: 359
Pitch size (100 – 120m^2)
Number of permanent annual pitches: 6
Area: 7 Total area (in hectares)
Altitude: 80m

Contact info

E-N 125 – Espiche, 8600 Luz/Lagos
Tel: +351 282789265
Fax: +351 282788578
Sat Nav: N 37º.65 W8º.43.56
Website: www.turiscampo.com

Campsite Orbitur Valverde*** (Algarve)

Campsite suitable for handicapped persons
Opening period: 01/01 up to and including 31/12
Price Guide: €32.00–€38.00
Number of touring pitches: 1000 (50 – 100m^2)
Number of permanent annual pitches: 100
Area: 10 Total area (in hectares)

Contact info

Estr. da Praia da Luz
8600-148 Lagos
Tel: +351 282789211-2
Fax: +351 282789213
Sat Nav N 37º.5.59 W 8º43.4

Campsite Obritur Quarteria*** (Eastern Algarve)

Open period: 01/01 up to including 31/12
Price Guide: €29.00–€35.00
Number of touring pitches: 1300 (60 – 130m^2)
Number of permanent annual pitches: 100
Area: 12 Total area (in hectares)

Contact info

Estrada da Fonte Santa
8125-618 Quarteira

Tel: +351 289302826
Fax: +351 289302822
Sat Nav: N 37º4.2 W 8º 5.14

Campsite Obritur Sagres** (Western Algarve)

Opening period: 01/01 up to and including 31/12
Price Guide: €28.00–€33.00
Number of touring pitches: 550 (40 – 100m^2)
Number of camper pitches: 70 à 70m^2
Area: 7 Total area (in hectares)

Contact info

Cerro das Moitas
8650-998 Vila de Sagres
Tel: +351 282624371
Fax: +351 282624445
Sat Nav: N37º1.22 W8º56.44

Parque de Armacoa de Pera*** (Central Algrarve)

Campsite suitable for handicapped persons
Opening period: 01/01 up to and including 31/12
Price Guide: €24.00–€30.40
Number of touring pitches: 650
Number of permanent annual pitches: 150
Area: 12 Total area (in hectares)

Contact info

EN. 269-1
8365-184 Armação de Pêra
Portugal
Tel: +351 282312260
Fax: +351 282315379
Sat Nav: N 37º 6.33 W 8º21.11

Camping Alvor-Dourada

Opening period: 01/01 up to and including 31/12
Price Guide: €21.50–€24.00
Number of touring pitches: 400
Number of permanent annual pitches: 50
Area: 4.5 Total area (in hectares)

Contact info

Estrada dos Montes
8500-053 Alvor Portimão
Portugal

Tel: +351 282459178
Fax: +351 282459178
Sat Nav: N 37º8.6 W 8º35.26

Parque de Campismo Calico* (Algarve)

Opening period: 01/01 up to and including 31/12
Price Guide: €18.00–€23.00
Number of touring pitches: 70
Number of permanent annual pitches: 60
Area: 10 Total area (in hectares)
Altitude: 200m

Contact info

Setio Caliço/Apartado 51
8901-907 Vila Nova de Caçela
Portugal
Tel: +351 281951195
Fax: +351 281951548
Sat Nav N 37º 11.11 W 7º33.0

Campsite Quinta de Odelouca (Algarve)

Opening period: 01/01 up to and including 31/12
Price Guide: €15.00–€19.00
Number of touring pitches: 30
Area: 2 Total area (in hectares)

Contact info

Vale Grande
8375-215 São Marcos da Serra
Portugal
Tel: +351 282361718
Sat Nav: N 37º20.22 W 8º22.20

Camping Olhao*** (Eastern Algarve)

Opening period: 01/01 up to and including 31/12
Price Guide: €37.00–€41.00
Number of touring pitches: 400 (50 – 110m^2)
Number of permanent annual pitches: 100
Area: 10 Total area (in hectares)

Contact info

Pinheiros de Marim/Ap 300
8700-914 Olhão
Portugal
Tel: +351 289700300

Fax: +351 289700390
Sat Nav: N 37º2.7 W 37º49.20

Parque Municipal de Camp, de Monte Gordo* (Eastern Algarve)

Opening period: 01/01 up to and including 31/12
Price Guide: €21.00–€24.00
Number of touring pitches: 500
Number of permanent annual pitches: 200
Area: 13.5 Total area (in hectares)#

Contact info

E.M. 511
8900 Vila Real de Santo António
Portugal
Tel: +351 281510970
Fax: +351 281510003
Sat Nav: N 37º 10.45 W 7º26.37

Campsite Turiscampo**** (Western Algarve)

Campsite suitable for handicapped persons
Opening period: 01/01 up to and including 31/12
Price Guide: €29.00–€35.00
Number of touring pitches: 359 (100 – 120m^2)
Number of permanent annual pitches: 6
Area: 7 Total area (in hectares)
Altitude: 80m

Contact info

E-N 125 – Espiche
8600 Luz/Lagos
Portugal
Tel: +351 282789265
Fax: +351 282788578
Sat Nav: N 37º6.5 W 8º43.56

P.C.da Fuseta** (Algarve)

Opening period: 01/01 up to and including 31/12
Price Giude: €16.00–€19.00
Number of touring pitches: 100
Number of permanent annual pitches: 100
Area: 3.3 Total area (in hectares)

Contact info

Rua da Liberdade 2/Ap.50
8700-908 Fuzeta
Portugal
Tel: +351 289793459
Fax: +351 289793285
Sat Nav: N 37º3.11 W 7º44.41

Public Transport

Buses for Algarve

This website provides information on bus travel in the Algarve, express buses running between the main towns of the Algarve as well as trips to Spain. Timetables and ticket prices are displayed in English.

www.eva-bus.com

Trains

This website displays timetables and prices in English; it is possible to travel from the Algarve to Lisbon in around two and a half hours.

www.cp.pt Tel: 351 707 210 202

Tagus river ferries

This website provides information on ferry crossings over the River Tagus. Information on river cruises is also available: this is ideal for taking a river cruise to see a different view of Lisbon; prices are around €20 for adults, €15 for children. The website is in Portuguese only.

www.transtejo.pt

Interesting Facts: Did you know?

Alliance. Portugal and England are the world's oldest alliance: they have a bond that exists closely even today. The alliance officially dates back to the 13th century, but as far back as 1147 the King of Portugal Afonso Henriques made the Englishman Gilbert of Hastings the Bishop of Lisbon. All through history, from fighting the Spanish armadas to Napoleon's invasion attempt and the Second World War, the two countries have remained close to this day. Queen Elizabeth II has had two state visits to Portugal: in 1957 and in 1985.

Bacalhau, (Dried Salt Cod). You will not have had a visit to Portugal without coming across Bacalhau; it is dried salt cod. For those not familiar with Bacalhau, it can be seen as not the most attractive dried flattened fish to buy. The Portuguese love it so much they have a different recipe for every day of the year: there are said to be over 1000 recipes in Portugal alone. It was invented over 500 years ago: when fishermen went further afield, they needed a way in which to preserve the catch for its long return journey home. Norway soon became the capital of producing and selling salted dried cod. Norway is still the largest exporter of dried cod to most of Europe. With Spain and Portugal having a 90% Roman Catholic population, salt cod became very popular on Fridays and over religious periods such as Lent, when it was forbidden to eat meat. The cod is soaked in water for up to three days; the water is changed two or three times a day to rehydrate the fish and remove the salt. Nowadays due to European laws restaurants are forbidden to use this type of salt cod and so buy the ready hydrated variety. If you have not tried a Bacalhau start off with the small Bacalhau pastels: they are small, deep fried and eaten as a snack.

Dried Salt cod

Bookshop, World's oldest: Portugal has the oldest recorded bookshop in the world, Livraria Bertrand. Founded in 1732, the book store has stood in the same place for 282 years. The shop was completely rebuilt after the original collapsed, along with most of Portugal, in the earthquake of 1755. The brand, now known as Bertrand today, has over 50 stores across the country.

Carob. Known in Portugal as the Alfarrobeira, this is more commonly known as the carob tree. Many people who have seen the carob often wonder what the green runner bean-like pods are that hang in bunches. The hanging pods turn black during the summer months when they are harvested; they are prized for many uses.

An interesting fact about the carob! Gold is graded in carats, as in 22ct, 18ct, 14ct, 9ct, but have you ever wondered how this came about? This goes as far back as Roman periods. When it came to the measuring of gold and precious gemstones, the Romans would use the hard seed from the carob pod as each seed weighed more or less the same. They had a gold coin called the solidus; it was weighed using the seeds. It took 24 carob seeds, which had a weight of 4.5 grams. Even today the British gold sovereign coin is 22ct and its weight comes from this early method. The carob pod and seed have many uses:

these include making chocolate substitute in diabetic foods and as emulsifiers and thickeners for food products, flour, and animal food. When black and left for about three months they become sweet and sticky, they can be eaten raw in this form.

Black dried Carob bean

Cork. Portugal is one of the largest producers of cork across the world. It supplies almost 50% of corks used in the wine industry. Known as the cork oak (Latin name: Quercus Sube), the tree is harvested every nine years. When the removal of the bark takes place it leaves the tree red in colour. Once stripped of its bark a number is then painted on for the year in which harvested.

Stacked cork left to dry in the sun

Today cork is still hand-harvested by skilled craftsmen who used a certain type of axe, and know just how deep to cut without harming the tree. This skill is passed down within families. No modern method has been found to successfully remove so much bark without harming the tree. There have been many attempts to use an alternative way to bottle wine, but even in recent years cork still holds as the traditional way to preserve wine into a vintage one.

On average it takes 10-15 years before a tree may be harvested for its first bark removal. Mature trees will yield 120 kilo of bark enough for around 4,000 bottles of wine.

Take a guess, what you would think is the age of the world's oldest living cork tree: 100, 500, 1,000 years old?

Well, if you consider that the world's oldest living olive tree, found in Loures, Portugal, is 2,850 years old, it may come as a surprise that the world's oldest living cork tree, also found in Portugal, is a mere 230 years old. This cork tree is nicknamed the whistler tree. Not impressed? Well perhaps you would be if you knew that this famous cork tree produced over 820 kilos of cork in just one harvest, enough to bottle 100,000 bottles of wine. Portugal's cork is so highly prized that Champagne producer Moët et Chandon mainly use Portuguese cork due to its dense quality. Cork is the world's longest-protected tree with records dating back to the 13th century. Even today it is illegal to harvest a tree that is too young. To chop down a cork oak requires permission from a government department; this applies to most of Europe.

Death Penalty. Portugal was the first country in the world to abolish the death penalty; the method used was hanging. Even though the last use of capital punishment in Portugal took place in Lagos in 1846, nearly 65 years passed until the death penalty was abolished for all crimes in Portugal in 1911.

Europe's longest bridge. The Vasco da Gama Bridge in Lisbon is a staggering 17.2 km or approximately 11 miles in length and 6 lanes wide. The bridge is such a secure structure that traffic is allowed to travel with speed up to 120 km/h or 75 mph. Construction started in in 1995; the bridge was completed and opened in 1998, in time to celebrate the 500th anniversary of the discovery of the sea route from Europe to India by Vasco da Gama. The bridge cost around €800 million. During construction the support pillars went down to a depth of 95 m. In 2014 it has been estimated that approximately 60,000 vehicles cross the bridge every day.

Football. This fact surprises many people: S.L.Benfica is the world's most supported football club, making an appearance in the well-known *Guinness Book of World Records* for having the largest number of fans for any single football club. It has an estimated 14 million worldwide supporters, and over 170,000 registered paying member supporters.

James Bond, 007. In 1952 when Ian Fleming was staying at his holiday home in Jamaica, the estate named Goldeneye (which also the title of the 17th Bond film (the first starring Pierce Brosnan. he started to write his first novel called *Casino Royale*; he based his book on a trip to Lisbon he had taken with a friend, a naval intelligence officer during World War Two. They visited Estoril where they both went to the famous casino there.

Fleming lost a lot of money to a Portuguese businessman, but claimed it was to a German spy, which it was not. This started the many fantasies that make up the book that became a bestseller and one of the James Bond films we know of today.

Language. Many people who come on holiday to Portugal will try to learn the odd word for their holiday. But what they may not know is that Portuguese is recognised as an international language: the fifth most spoken language in the world and the third most spoken in Europe after English and Spanish. It Is spoken worldwide by over 250 million people and is the official language of Portugal, Brazil, Angola, and Mozambique.

Pastel de Nata (Custard Tart). Portugal is famous for a small custard tart called the Pastel de Nata. This is believed to date back to the early 18th century, and is said to have been created by Catholic monks as an extra means of income. Originally called Pastel de Belem, the tarts soon proved very popular in the early 19th century, by which time many had started to make their own version of the tart. They become known as Pastel de Nata. It was not long before they spread to other countries including China, who quickly saw many other uses for the flaky pastry. Today it is known as Massa Tenra: you would know it as the crispy pastry of a Chinese spring roll.

Famous Pastel da Nata

One baker in Lisbon makes 10,000 Pastel de Nata every day. With people queuing for these delicious tartlets you will not find a café or baker across the whole of the Portugal who does not sell them. It is said that up to half a million are consumed every day.

Spices, Piri Piri. In the 16th century Portugal was the largest trader of spices in the world. Portugal had discovered an easy route to India, with its black peppercorns; it soon became one of the largest controllers of the trade in black peppercorns. These had nearly the same value as gold at the time; this soon dwindled when other countries started to grow peppers. The Portuguese appear to have been the first traders to spread the chilli pepper globally. Chilli originated from South America; Portugal introduced chilli to India in 1498. Soon the chilli pepper became easy to cultivate, with countries like Angola and Mozambique using the chilli in many ways. Today Portugal is famous for its chicken piri piri which is said to have originally come from Mozambique. Portugal remains one of Europe's largest consumers of chicken.

Piri Piri hot peppers

A-Z Beach Information for the Algarve

Two of Portugal's four sides are flanked by the Atlantic Ocean; Portugal has 800 kilometres of breathtaking coastline and around 80 beaches in the Algarve alone, with many hidden coves. It would take the average visitor many visits to be able to say "Been there, done that."

Portugal's coastlines are so varied that different climates are found in the different areas of the country. When venturing off to the smaller coves care should be taken due to possible rock fall and lack of lifeguards. Many beaches that have possible rock fall are highlighted with yellow/black warning signs.

The beach offers many water sports for real enthusiasts or just hiring a pedalo for a family day out.

Portugal has moved into the 21st century with many beaches patrolled by land and sea for your safety, and huge improvements for disabled access.

Portuguese are more laid-back when it comes to beach life and are often found reading or playing cards in family groups. You can often hear the tinkle of a bell ringing as the locals sell the well-known doughnut-type cake called Malassadas. These are sold on the beaches from licensed sellers. Any water sport events are also required to have a licence and complaints book.

Note: many beaches will offer sunbeds and shades; these are known as concessions and have to include a life guard. The beach areas in front of the sunbed are also part of the concession. If you set up brollies or beach mats, you may be asked to move from this area, as the sunbed owners will have paid a licence for this area of the beach. Often many people will sunbathe topless; unless the beach is designated as a naturist beach you may be ask to cover up by the maritime police.

Albanderia (Central Algarve) is a small, pretty beach ideal for those who don't mind a short climb. Next door to the Benagil beach this is a two-part beach surrounded by cliffs.

Alvor (Western Algarve) has a large beach in front of the village. Alvor beach fringes on the eastern half of Lagos Bay and has no cliffs. This beach has easy access, with many sand dunes which have developed from the winds over time. It is a popular beach for wind surfers and hosts numerous water sports. Fishing from the beach in summer months is not permitted.

Armacao de Pera (Central Algarve) is a large flat beach with one end towards the east at the start of the cliff tops. It has many caves that can be seen by taking a short trip in a traditional Algarve fishing boat for just a few euros. The large beach has easy access and also has wooden decking boards for wheelchair/pushchair access. Armacao de Pera beach is popular with the Portuguese who holiday from Lisbon.

This beach is great for long walks as it is less than 20 minutes' walk to Albufeira. Towards the east the beach still boasts its fishing community. In the mornings you can often buy fish straight from the fishermen as they pull the boats up onto the beach to unload. Overall this is a good family beach, with nearby bars right on the beach; prices for a coffee or small beer are low at around €1.20 (price at Pedro's bar in 2014).

Arrifana (Western Algarve): south of Ajezur, this beach is one of the very few which is right next to the little village, with good access.

Amoreira (Western Algarve): this beach is north of Aljezur on the main road near the campsite. The road is a dead end road with parking overlooking the beach, which is large with plenty of space. It is busy in peak season, but like most beaches it is peaceful and good for walking in the quieter months. There is a river estuary at the far end and this is perhaps the safer part with warmer water, as the current on the main beach can be unpredictable.

Batata (Western Algarve): down near Lagos, this small beach has the remains of small fort, clear sand and jetties going out to sea at the entrance of a small harbour.

Burgau is today still a well-known fishing village, with its small boats scattered on the beach, known locally as fisherman's beach and quarry beach. This is a small, golden sandy beach with easy access via steps or ramp, flanked by low-lying cliffs giving ideal protection from the coastal breeze. The water here is generally calm and the quality excellent. It is reached by following the village's cobbled streets down to the waterfront where it has a wooden beach walkway. Even in peak season the beach does not get too overcrowded, although parking can be a bit of a problem. Plenty of parking can be found on the outskirts of the village and when you wander down the narrow streets you get a feel of an old Cornish village.

Burgau beach

Benagil (Central Algarve): to get to this beach, turn off at the traffic lights on the EN125 near the International School. It offers good parking with the beach being a few metres away. Backed by rocks this small beach has the golden sands that you want for a quiet day out. It offers picnic tables often used by fisherman who fish from the tops of the rocks.

Caneriros (Western Algarve) is a bit further east from Ferragudo. Located down a cul-de-sac road, it is a good-sized beach, popular for its flanked cliffs which offer shady places in the afternoons. Access to the beach is easy but lack of parking means roadside parking; be careful where you park to avoid fines.

Carvoeiro (Central Algarve): a pretty beach right in front of the central square with many bars and cafés towards the beach's main entrance. Due to the small size of the beach it can get crowded in peak season. Heading out towards Rocha Brava, Centianes beach is a short distance away. Carvoeiro beach features on many postcards and is popular with photographers. Walking or driving up the steep hill towards Sesmarinas gets you to the other part of Cavalho beach. This is reached by steep steps down to the bottom, but is well worth the effort even if just for a photo opportunity.

Continue further up the road and you will come to a restaurant with a small car park and steps taking you down to a small beach, Paraiso. Due to the steepness this is not suitable for young children, fragile adults, or those with disability problems.

Castelo (Central Algarve) is approached from a short stretch of track from the parking area with a few steps. Nothing too arduous, this leads down to a well sheltered beach flanked by low cliffs. This is located on the old Albufeira and Pera road and is well signposted.

Castelejo (Western Algarve): one of the few beaches on the west coast where it is relatively safe to swim due to the less dangerous underlying currents. This beach is located to the north-west of the small town of Vila do Bispo. It is one of the smaller beaches and has a completely different atmosphere to those found on the southern coastline. It may not suit everyone but those that do visit tend to return.

Gale (Central Algarve): a picture postcard beach that is popular in peak season, well signposted so easy to reach. It has a large car park and bar/restaurant. It is a split beach with one side having rocks that you can clamber over, which is very popular during the winter months with surfers, whilst the other half of the beach is ideal for relaxing. New wooden decking runs along the beach, giving easy access for pushchairs or mobility difficulties. Sun loungers can be hired in the peak season.

Garrao (Eastern Algarve): one of the main beaches in the well-known Algarve golden triangle. Originally before any development this was a quiet beach with small wooded areas of mainly pine trees. Vale do Lobo and the adjoining Quinta do Lago developed in the 1960s, with a nearby riding school. It is possible to ride along the beach. Praia de Garrao lies between these two resorts and features private areas offering sun-loungers and shades. There is a large part open to the general public, offering the finest beachside restaurants in the Algarve.

Lagoa (Central Algarve): this cove is located near Novotel Vermar, with many beach bars all year long, some serving snacks. The beach is popular in the summer, but calm during winter. Being so flat it is a great beach for winter walkers; the beach's sand has an almost white appearance and very few rocks. During low tide, immersed rocks become visible.

Marinha Beach, Lagoa

Lagos (Western Algarve): to the east of Lagos sits the largest and main beach Meia Praia. With golden sands offering a good choice of water sports, Lagos has the calmest waters for snorkelling. On the sands in high season volleyball courts are set up on the beach as well as football. These games always welcome you if you want to join in.

Restaurants and beach bars are situated close by. Meia Praia is a wide sandy beach bay with character and has low sand dunes. The beach is about four kilometres long. If you want to find the many nearby smaller beaches then Batata is a good example. Follow the road from Lagos towards the marina. Meia Praia is well signposted and has good access for all.

Lagos Marina

Mareta (Western Algarve): a sunbather's wishlist beach, right in front of the village of Sagres. This is a sheltered beach away from the winds and offers less water sport than many of the other beaches in western Algarve. There is good access. One for relaxing with a good book.

Marinha (Central Algarve): Just a little further up from Benagil, this is a quiet picture postcard beach nestled down below from the cliff tops, offering quite a long stretch of beach and shallow waters. Care should be taken as the bottom sea plate is rocky. It offers good shelter in the afternoon when the sun swings around at the far end of the beach.

Martinhal (Western Algarve) is one of the beaches off the Sagres bay. Well-known to windsurfers, this beach is located just outside the village of Sagres toward the end of the bay.

Monte Clerigo is one of those beaches that when the tide goes out will give hours of fun exploring the many little rock pools that children so like to explore. But it offers a good excuse for the adults as well, as it has a large sand area. The beach is also a good one for amateur snorkel lovers.

Monte Gordo (Eastern Algarve), almost on the Spanish border, is a large developed town with an amazingly long and deep beach. It is busy in peak season, but there is always plenty of space to find a spot. You will find the water a little warmer than most of the Algarve due to being close to the Mediterranean. This is one for the family as it offers the normal range of cafés, ice creams, and the usual shops selling beach toys. Wooden decking allows easy access for disabled or pushchairs.

Monte Gordo beach with good wheelchair access

Odeceixe is in the northwest corner of the Algarve in the northern parish of Aljezur. This is one of the few official naturist beaches in Portugal, with a flat beach and clear golden sand. The tip joins the Atlantic via the river Seixe, almost making it seem like an island. It is a lovely, quiet and relaxing beach that sits in a cove surrounded by black and white granite rocks.

Praia Grande (Western Algarve) is a large beach just off Ferragudo where the estuary Arade meets the sea. It offers views of the Santa Catarina fort down towards Praia da Rocha. Praia Grande is a good location for all-round water sports facilities.

Praia da luz (Western Algarve): the beachfront at Praia da Luz has a lovely traditional cobbled walkway, using the different colour cobbles to create art in the pavement. The beach can be promenaded along the walkway, which is popular with locals for evening strolls. The beach is a large crescent-shaped bay with soft white sand. At the far end of the beach sit the dark stone rock cliffs.

At the far end of the beach you can find plenty of rock pools at low tide, great for the kids. There are plenty of water sports on offer in high season (check they are licensed). Access onto the beach is very good for all. There are several beach restaurants and snack-bars to choose from, many located on the beach. Many small shops sell souvenirs and beach toys. Praia da Luz is a popular beach with families; the waters are calm, good for swimming.

The cliffs of Praia da Luz

Srª de Rocha (Central Algarve) has the best of both worlds and is a hidden gem.

It is located off the N269-1 between Armacao de Pera and Porches: if heading towards Porches a turning opposite the petrol station will lead down to Srº de Rocha. It is best to park at the top near the old chapel: there you will look down on two beaches. One has a restaurant and fishing boats; the other is a quiet beach with signs of fallen rock. A man-made 18th-century tunnel, about 100m in length, joins the two beaches. Access through the tunnel can be restricted during high tide. Fishermen offer cave trips; the water can be crystal clear which make it popular with snorkelers. There are two dedicated disabled parking spaces at the bottom of the beach, as well as a public toilet baby changing room and showers that give hot water for a small charge in the meter.

Places to Visit

Central Algarve

Albufeira

Albufeira is the main coastal district in Central Algarve. It is one of the most popular places to visit for young families and single youngsters, due to the night life with many bars and restaurants. Albufeira contains many places of interest to visit for those who are looking beyond nightclubs, with museums, churches, galleries and flea markets. Albufeira remains the main tourist destination for Central Algarve due to its coastal location. It is just a 35-minute drive from the main airport of Faro.

The parishes within proximity of Albufeira include Guia, a quaint village that has become well known for celebrated medal- and award-winning wines. The winery owned by Sir Cliff Richard is Adega do Cantor. Nearby are Ferreira's, Olhao de Aqua, and Paderne with a castle sitting on the top of the village. The architecture of Albufeira ranges from typically Algarvian narrow streets with pale white and sometimes tiled houses, to modern tourist developments. Apartments near the newly built marina can be seen from many parts of Albufeira due to the bright vivid pinks, blues, and yellows of the houses: It is dubbed "Legoland" by the locals. Nightlife on the strip, located near the Montechoro section of Albufeira, proves popular during the summer with all ages, especially the younger tourists. Going towards the strip the most popular bars often stay open until 4-6 am. Nightclubs, cafés, and snack bars are abundant. Since 2011 the prices have reduced due to the European recession.

Everything is more expensive here: a Galao (latte-style coffee), always served in a tall glass, can be €2.50, while inland it costs around 90 cents. Meals are often cheaper, from as little as €4.50 for mixed grill or omelette and chips in the many snack bars, but expect to pay around €15 per head for a restaurant meal off the main menu. Albufeira has everything you could want for a holiday, without the need for car hire. Those wanting to see the real Algarve have a good choice of excursions, with buses covering the whole of the region. Albufeira old town has a more relaxed feeling, and has a central square decorated with trees and colourful shrubs. It contains many street cafés, bars, and restaurants for a quiet meal or a cool drink. The streets leading off the square offer many sorts with clothes shops, leather goods gift shops, street stalls and many mini supermarkets for daily necessities. On the outskirt of Albufeira to the east is Olhos d'Agua. It bears a resemblance to Albufeira but is more popular with the older generation, having many four star hotels and plentiful restaurants.

Lightlife in Albufeira

Alcantarilha

Alcantarilha in the Central Algarve comes under the district of Silves; this small village has grown in size in the last ten years, with the EN125 road running through it. The old part of the village remains little changed, with narrow streets, and the main high street which runs the length of the village. The road narrows to just one car wide near the large and impressive church.

Attached to the church at one side is small bone chapel, opened every day, Skulls and bones cover the walls and ceiling. It is large enough for two to three people to stand and gaze in amazement at such a wonder; there is no macabre feel about the chapel considering human bones are on display. You will find it well worth walking around the village. Down the back roads you will stumble upon an early dwelling dating back to the 17th century. Walking around the rear of the property, the old garden wall has original arrow slits from which to fire arrows upon unwanted intruders. Continue and the alley will bring you back to the main high street.

Alcantarilha village has much to offer throughout the year, holding a monthly market near the ambulance/fire station. It also holds a monthly flea market in the same location. The village holds annual events, including a dried fruits event which goes on with live music and entertainment into the evening. The festival is predominately local produce of handmade sweets, cakes, dried fruits, liqueurs, and other handmade crafts traditional to the Algarve and Portugal. There is also a small living museum that is set up for the duration of the festival showing what life was like there in the 19th and early 20th centuries. The fair is normally held on the first week of September. On the village green can also be found an old Nora. This early well was driven by a harnessed donkey which walked around the Nora to draw up water for drinking and washing. Opposite is a building which holds a daily fish and produce market. Stalls are arranged in a quadrangle, leaving the centre open to the elements.

The village offers a good range of restaurants that are well worth a visit, serving locally caught fish from Armacao de Pera. You may even see the scouts often holding meetings in the village hall; they can be heard and seen with band practice and marches. On one of the back streets is a small museum which shows different farm implements and other early household items used in past years. The newer part of the extended village consists of new houses built on the other side of the EN125 road. There is an Aldi supermarket and a small retail park.

If going to the nearby town of Armacao de Pera then this village is well worth stopping off to explore. Villages like this are the hidden gems of the Algarve.

Algoz village highest point

Algoz

The growing village of Algoz is within the District of Silves. Just 7 km away is the nearby City of Armacao de Pera, with a golden beach that is the longest in the Central Algarve. Algoz originates from the Arabic word "Al-Gûzz" which derives from the name of a war-like Asian tribe from the Middle East, dating back to the 12th century.

The past history of Algoz is macabre. Towns and villages whose names start with 'Al' date from the Moorish period. In history Algoz was known for executions, but no such evidence exists today. Algoz has grown in popularity. The village hosts many events throughout the year and is best known for having the largest monthly market in the Central Algarve (see market dates). This is spread over a large area to the side of the village hall, which has a small playground in front, and is a very traditional market, unlike others aimed at tourists.

The Village has two banks with ATMs, as well a good choice of shops and a daily fish and fruit market. Algoz boasts ten different restaurants. Most offer a Prata da Dia (dish of the day) with a three-course meal with wine costing under €8. Restaurants tend to get busy with local workers, at midday to 3pm.

Walk around the village and you will find houses boasting elaborate stone carving on parapet walls and windows, showing that the village had wealth from trading merchants who lived there.

Old oil presses and stone troughs sit along the grass verge with a small picnic area that can be found on the road towards Silves. Further along stands the public open air laundry, built in 1933 but closed in the 1990s. In the village centre sits a picturesque church with clock tower and cockerel weathervane. The village has a patron saint, Our Lady of Mercy, whilst in the village centre sit four granite grinding stones used in the olive oil pressing industry.

To the south of Algoz, sitting on the village's highest hill, is the Chapel of Nossa Senhora do Pilar, with fine views across the village and sea views of Armacao de Pera.

A fair is held twice a year: on the 10th August, the day of Sâo Miguel; and the day of São Luís on the last Sunday in September. There are also local horse and carriage meetings held in the village near the village hall, with a pig roast and other food snacks on offer.

Just 1 km on the outskirts of the village, heading towards Ferrerias and Tunes on the EN269, is a very traditional Portuguese tea shop: Quinta dos Avos. This includes a horse cart museum with free admission, which is open on Saturdays only. The tea shop is open every day except Tuesdays, from 2pm until 7pm. For those with GPS its coordinates are N.37°.09.21 – W.08° 17.09.

For those looking to stay in the village it offers a few guest houses. Four kilometres outside the village is Krazy World with reptiles, petting animals, mini golf, and a large swimming pool. Families can spend a day enjoying the facilities. In 2013 changes in Portuguese law saw many village/town halls combine, to cut back on running fees. The village of Tunes now shares the village hall located in Algoz. A village hall is also known as a Freguesia.

Almancil

Almancil in the Eastern Algarve comes under the district of Loulé with nearby Vale do Lobo and Quinta do Largo. Nicknamed the Golden Triangle, this is one of the most expensive areas of the Algarve. What is a shame is that whilst houses can sell for well into the millions, the town of Almancil seems to be forgotten from the tourist map.

Many books mention the 18th century church, of Sao Lourence (Saint Lawrence), which sits on the outskirts of the town with the EN125 dual carriageway running along the side. The church, with its spectacular hand-painted tile interior and hand-carved wooden gilded altar, appears on many postcards. The church is one of the Algarve's treasured monuments: it has survived many earthquakes, including the devastating one of 1755 which destroyed most of Portugal. At the bottom of the hill in Sao Lourenco is an Antiques shop with many things of interest (English speaking). Near the church is the art gallery Rastro, with free entrance, displaying many international artists.

The main town of Almancil has a long main street, with many good restaurants and plenty of interesting shops. It has antique and interior design shops located off the main high street. You will also find an English bookshop. When heading out of Almancil along the back road towards Quarteira, there are many good shops which offer handmade tiles made and painted using the area's traditional methods of tile production.

There is a layby picnic area, with an old water Nora. These were pulled round in a circle by donkeys to draw up water from the well. The hand painted tiles that decorate the layby show scenes of life in olden days. It is hard not to see that the large palatial houses in the area each stick to their own unique architectural design. The nearby Vale do Lobo is the nearest beach for Almancil, along with nearby golf courses and a nature park.

Almancil has a large water park with some of the largest water slides in the Algarve and is popular with families. Almancil holds two monthly fresh produce markets and two monthly flea/ antique markets, popular with those looking for a bargain to take home. Located off Almancil's main high street is a large landscaped park.

Alte, set in Central Algarve, comes under the district parish of Loulé. It is famous with the Portuguese for natural spring waters which run 365 days a year. Whilst the village is set inland amongst the hills, Alte sits in a basin surrounded by undisturbed countryside.

Entering Alte from the west along the main N124 road, the first thing seen is the main churchyard along with a newish roundabout, with a large car park off one of the exits. Alte has the main road that more or less circles the town. There is a bridge which narrows to one car width that crosses the river. This is a popular spot with locals and tourist as the river has wild ducks and geese, with fresh running spring water which comes out of two clay pipes. Often this is busy, with locals who fill their bottles with drinking water. A sign reads that it is not tested and not for drinking, but this sadly is part of the health and safety laws that have hit Europe; the sign is to cover such laws.

This river bank has stone tables and benches used for picnics by the river's edge. In May the village holds a festival of marriage and a food and music festival.

Alte's famous poet Candido Pacheco has a monument dedicated to his work, with blue and white tiles showing sonnets written by him. Born in the 1870s, Pacheco is part of the village's proud history. A brown sign shows directions to the fontes, which Alte is famous for. These are well worth the walk in the summer months. Weekends get busy with families who picnic and swim in the crystal clear running waters. The friendly atmosphere is tangible: it is a good place to sit and just enjoy the fun being had. A bar/restaurant located on the other side of the wooden bridge.

Alte has plenty to offer with bars, cafés, and restaurants. There are many shops, including a supermarket that sadly has a large sign to show its position in bright colours. It spoils the village which has stood the test of time, and tradition.

Alte has two churches. The main one is in the centre and sits impressively looking over the village centre, with its impressive doorway and hand-carved stone archways. There is a plaque that gives you the history of it. Alte sees safari jeeps filled with tourists looking for the 'real' Algarve. Yet to just drive through the village is a shame, as Alte has so much to offer: hidden backstreets highlighted with colour from bougainvilleas. Alte holds a very good carnival in February, when the rest of Portugal and the Algarve celebrate this season too.

Alte

Armacao de Pera

Armacao de Pera in central Algarve falls under the district parish of Silves. It is famous for its fishing industry from the days when tuna was plentiful. Armacao de Pera still to this day thrives with fishing boats that come in daily and unload their catch on the fisherman's beach. You can often buy fresh fish and crab direct from the fisherman as they unload their nets or watch the auction (loto) next to the Red Cross building. The days of the small village have long since gone: it became a town (vila) in 1996. It is steeped in history, with remains of its fort along the seafront; the original coat of arms remains unscathed on the 17th-century fort entrance. However, many would not even know it was a fort, as little sign of this remains unless viewed from the beach. Until 2009 part of it was used as the main police station and jail. Sitting in the middle of the fort is the 17th-century small chapel of Santo Antonio.

Armacao de Pera underwent €9 million improvements along its seafront to bring it in line with modern living. There is good wheelchair access to most places. It holds traditional artesian fairs along the front with handmade jewellery, stained glass and pottery from nearby Porches in the old casino café, which dates from the 1930s and is now part-art gallery and part-local tourist office.

Outside the tourist office is free Wi-Fi, and new play area for children, with soft safety flooring. Take note of the coloured cobblestones laid in the pavement: you will notice playing cards and dice, following the theme of the old casino building. You will see the pattern in the cobbles change to fish and fishing nets near the Holiday Inn hotel.

Whilst the town has many high-rise apartments, it lacks a main high street of shops, unlike other towns. It is well worth a visit for its main church in the square that rings out on the hour. Many backstreets still offer traditional cuisine in the many restaurants. It has to be said it has one of the longest golden beaches in central Algarve. This can be entered on the flat from the fisherman's beach end or a few steps down at the far end. If you are looking for no-frills town, then Armacao de Pera is it.

Many Portuguese from Lisbon holiday here. There is a large daily fresh fish and fruit and veg market, as well as a street market every Saturday and Wednesday outside the post office. There are many mini supermarkets where you can get nearly everything; hence the town has grown in popularity.

This is what keeps its bars and restaurants more traditional: Armacao de Pera has fewer bars and pubs, with lower-key and higher standards than those fighting for trade in nearby Albufeira. Prices are more realistic: a coffee or beer on the seafront only costs €1.20. Restaurants offer a tourist menu with the starter, main and sweet courses along with wine for around €10-15; this was still the case in 2014. Overall this is a great town for walking, being mainly on the flat. Armacao de Pera still retains its tiny cottages hidden away on the backstreets near fisherman's beach.

The town's love of modern art can be seen on many roundabouts along the main road toward Porches. Note: the bar/cafe on the beach on fisherman's beach is an official public toilet with a ramp for disabled people. You do need to ask for the key: the toilet is only open to the public in peak season, from 1st June until 30th September.

Benafim Grande

Benafim Grande in the Central Algarve is located on the EN124 road, running from Alcoutim on the Spanish border, towards Silves in the Central Algarve. Being over 200 metres above sea level and set in the Serra de Caldeirao hills, Benafim enjoys coastal views from the top at the church.

The church has a small clock tower and at the rear of the church are hand-painted tiles of Christ on the cross dating from the 18th century. The whole feel of Benafim is a true encounter with how the Portuguese lived, from the grander merchant houses to the humble stone-built houses that are just six feet wide with a small doorway and one window. These were built with pride with many having large fancy chimneys for which the Algarve is famous.

Benafim comes under the district of Loulé, one of the richest parishes in the Algarve. The town's public places have been restored whilst keeping all its charm. Many narrow cobblestone streets have not changed for decades; the main street is wide, with benches every fifty metres along with old style street lamps.

Towards the rear of the town is a local tiled water font now fully restored which boasts scenes of the past with hand-painted blue and white tiles. The font is now updated and fitted with brass taps that replaced the stone gully that used to flow continuously with spring water. The water is suitable for drinking and used by the locals. Just a short distance away is the fully restored and working public open air laundry housing public toilets. The main wall has artistic scene of an Arab man with a young girl, painted in 1996.

Across the road is a picnic area with an old water Nora, with wooden tables and benches as well as a stone-built barbecue. There is an information stand showing areas of interest within the town and also a small museum. The area is very popular with walking groups with routes that can be seen on Google Earth. One route runs through Rocha da Pena: signs kindly ask you not to make too much noise due to the wildlife population that breeds in the nature reserve. The walk is about three hours depending on your pace, and covers less than 5km. You will often see shepherds as the area is known for the grazing of goats and sheep. The lime soil is one of the largest in the Algarve for the growing of almonds and figs.

Benafim Grande has all you could want if staying nearby: a large supermarket on the entrance on the EN124, with a petrol station; a chemist, a medical centre, a sports club. There are plenty of small bars and a few restaurants that serve traditional Portuguese dishes, as well as the dish of the day (Prata da Dia). Benafim Grande holds an annual event normally on the 3rd of October with runs until the 5th Republic day for Portugal. Locals pull out all the stops, with family and friends meeting at the local picnic and barbecue area.

Boliqueime

Boliqueime, in the Central Algarve, is a small village that comes under the district of Loulé. The Algarve is famous for its chimneys which are unique to this part of Portugal. They come in all shapes and sizes and are featured on many postcards.

It is said that the larger and more elaborate the chimney, the more wealth one had. You will often see grand chimneys on small cottages that look out of proportion. The small village of Boliqueime celebrates this by having a chimney on its coat of arms. The village has the largest cement factory in the Algarve and can be seen from the A22 motorway. Boliqueime sits at around 45 meters above sea level with good sea views.

The small square at the village centre, with the main church being the dominant building in the centre, was completely rebuilt after the 1755 earthquake.

There are many narrow streets that still have cobblestones. Boliqueime has remnants of its past wealth, with evidence of merchants' houses with stone door surrounds, wrought iron balconies and window grills.

Many tourists would not find a reason to visit the village, but Boliqueime has two smaller parishes. One is Fonte de Boliqueime, with the EN125 road running through the middle of it. You will not actually find Fonte de Boliqueime. The place name refers to hot and cold springs that were present in the 13th to 15th century. Nowadays the only remaining evidence of a fonte is one that sits inside a restaurant.

Poco de Boliqueime is just further up. Most tourists who come here think that they have visited Boliqueime and that it has nothing to offer. But they would be wrong: if they drove that little further until they reached Boliqueime itself, they would see that the village has the charm of other villages in the Algarve. Boliqueime has a monthly market on the last Thursday of the month (see Markets) and many good restaurants offering fantastic sunset views. The village is well worth the inland visit for those staying closer to the coast. Boliqueime village holds food events in August September in honor of Our Lady of Sorrows, normally held over a two-day weekend.

Guia

Guia in the Central Algarve is a small village that comes under the district of Albufeira, being just 4 kilometers away. Guia today has become famous across Portugal for its chicken piri-piri and wine production. In the 16th century when Portugal discovered the spice it was a huge trading tool with other countries. It was in fact Portugal that introduced hot spices to India. Chicken piri-piri is believed to have originated from Angola and Mozambique, but nowadays it is one of Portugal's national dishes, with Portugal being the largest consumers of chicken in Europe.

The village of Guia in the past played an important part of the Algarve. The windmills of the village and that of the nearby village of Algoz were well known within the milling industry. The windmill is incorporated in the coat of arms for the village. It still has a well preserved windmill that sits in the grounds of the vineyards Adega da Cantor. This name translates as 'the winery of the singer' and is the name given to it by the well-known English singer Sir Cliff Richard, who has developed many award-winning wines from the vineyard, which he started from scratch. The vineyard now offers tours and wine tastings at its nearby shop at the rear of the Algarve shopping centre.

The village is now so associated with chicken piri-piri and wine that they have dedicated a roundabout with sculptures of wine bottles and chickens.

The village is a good stop-off point as it has much to offer. It has a good daily covered market for fish and plenty of restaurants. The village offers ample parking just off the main high street; it is well worth strolling around the many backstreets full of cottages with their brightly coloured frontages, to the grander merchants' houses with carved stone door and window surrounds, and fancy wrought iron Juliet balconies. The main high street has a good selection of café/bars as well as ATM machines. There is a small chapel with a Moorish-style courtyard garden which is well worth a look. The village has a picnic park with the old Nora waterwell dating from the 1940s that used to serve the local community.

The village splits into two with the EN125 running through it; on the other part of the village is one of the largest piri-piri restaurants in Portugal, seating around 800. It can be found on the road to Algoz. There are nearby beaches of Gale and Albufeira with their many rugged rock formations that feature in many postcards, as well as some stunning golden beaches that Algarve has become known for, having some of the best voted beaches in Europe.

Loulé

The city of Loulé in Central Algarve has a very cosmopolitan feel and is nicknamed the Golden Triangle. The main municipal council for Vilamoura makes it one of the richest in the region, it has few palm trees but very green, tree-lined avenues with a café culture. The main street, José da Costa Mealha, has a small parkland strip running through the centre, with park benches and a bandstand with marble sculptures. There are small kiosks where you can sit and have coffee; whilst traffic and people are all around you, it still gives a calming atmosphere to relax.

Loulé is famous for its Saturday markets that can bring hustle and bustle to the city,

Parking in the city can be near impossible in the summer months. This is also true in the carnival season as Loulé Carnival is one of the biggest events in the city and is famous across the Algarve with floats coming from Brazil. It takes places in February or March and runs for three days; the third day is Shrove Tuesday.

Loulé has many shops found among back lanes. It is a large city offering most things of interest including galleries, a public swimming pool, chapels, and museums.

The daily market is held six days a week in a Moorish-style building, looking as though it belongs more in Morocco than Portugal. All are within easy walking distance from the city centre.

On the historical side Loulé has a castle dating back to the 12th Century. The Arab moors' castle has been virtually destroyed, leaving some walls still standing that are now surrounded by modern buildings. Like most other towns in Portugal, most of the older buildings were destroyed in the earthquake that occurred in 1755.

Gothic arches and side chapels dating from the 16th century have survived; they can be found in the backstreets, with gift shops selling copperware, leather, cane, and wooden items. There is a museum that is devoted to the local industry of dried fruits. It is interesting to see how these products are prepared for storage. To the west of the town is a hilltop church that is built on the site of a 16th-century chapel. Its dome roof can be seen from the A22 motorway. This is the destination of an annual religious procession with the shrines carried through the streets in processions.

Overall Loulé has much to offer, with two markets, one of which is a gypsy market aimed at tourism and ideal for families. The city is more of a grown-up, café-based, cultured place, appearing quiet on some days without the hustle and bustle one expects from a city. Check with the tourist office to see what events are on: even if the dried fruits fair may sound unappealing, you would miss out on the music and dancing that go with it. When other events are on, the city can spring into action, making great family days out.

NOTE: Parking is pay and display from short stays of 20 cents for 15 minutes to all day; tow away is in operation if you fail to pay at the nearby meters.

Paderne

Paderne in the Central Algarve is a small village that sits just 7 kilometres from the parish town of Albufeira. Whilst it remains one of the small villages not on the tourist trail, Paderne is well worth adding to places to visit whilst in Portugal.

The village has a castle dating back to the 12th century: this is one of the castles on the national flag of Portugal.

Paderne boasts a fully intact Roman bridge: this was not seen as being important until the 1860s, when restoration started. Today it has the status as an ancient monument. Unless you are a serious walker, it is better to visit the castle by car or bike. On the same road heading towards the castle from Paderne there is a natural spring set in a large square, still in use today with people from surrounding areas collecting the drinking water. It is often frequented by gypsies with their horses and carts. Paderne has a public laundry with around 18 stone troughs with scrubbing boards under a wooden tiled open building. It may seem strange to see, but the water flowing for the public laundry flows away from the main drinking water spring outlets. The river flows towards the park area with public information boards about the surroundings.

Once a year locals from Paderne and nearby Alfontes battle it out in a mini water sports day with canoe races, all ending with a joint effort of a BBQ and a well-earned beer along the riverbank. During the rest of the year, this is a great place to take a picnic and enjoy the river, whilst nearby trees offer shelter in the hotter summer months.

Heading back to the main village, the church sits in the village centre. As Paderne is all uphill, with its many backstreets that are narrow, make sure you pay attention to the road signs: many small streets are either one way or no entry unless GNR (resident). It is well worth visiting the church (Nossa Senhora da Esperanca) in the small square dating from the 15th century. This has had plenty of rebuilds with a later extension; the carvings inside are from the 17th-18th century and form part of the church's priceless history. The village offers good parking at the bottom, near a bronze statue of a tuba player.

There are many bars/restaurants offering the dish of the day. The village holds different events throughout the year as well as a monthly market held on the 1st Saturday of the month. Paderne also holds a recreation of a medieval fair in December/January.

Pera

Pera in Central Algarve comes under the district of Silves. Little is known about the history of the village. The name means pear ('piro' in Latin). Pera is now more associated with the larger city of Armacao de Pera, well known for its fishing industry.

In the $16^{th} - 18^{th}$ centuries Pera was well known for its sandy soil, which was ideal for growing pears. These were used in preserves and marmalade, as the variety was not suitable for eating, only cooking. The pears were also dried in the sun as a dried fruit, along with carob and grape.

The reason for mentioning this is that the neighbouring village of Alcantarilha holds an annual dried fruits fair in the first week in September, with many stalls selling foods consisting of dried fruits in all forms. There is a fun side to the festival with live music until late as well as stalls selling home-cooked food followed with a glass of the local wine.

The village of Pera even has the carob and grape on the coat of arms. Pera as a village has many single cobblestone streets only one car in width.

The village has two churches, the main one (Nossa Senhora do Rosario) dating from the 18th Century. Sitting on the highest point, this gives great views of the coast and the large town of Armacao de Pera. The barren-looking land between is called Salgardos, a well-known nature reserve that sits on salt marshes, very popular with bird watchers, with many different bird varieties including the flamingo.

The village has a good daily indoor fish and produce market, plenty of small shops and banks, as well as numerous bars and restaurants where a dish of the day can still be had for around €7-8. Pera has expanded in the last few years with a modern housing estate on the outer edge towards the Albufeira side.

Pera is perhaps now more known for its sand Fiesa (sand sculpture festival). Now in its 12th year (2014), it boasts to be the largest in Europe, with a different theme each year. Also just up the road is Real Picadeiro, a horse-riding centre, with regular shows as well as a restaurant open in the evenings with themed nights including fado (traditional Portuguese singing).

Porches

Porches in the Central Algarve comes under the district of Lagoa; the village can be seen from the EN125 with the main church being dominant, sitting on the top of the hill.

Porches played an important part as a look-out in the Roman period due to its high point with views of the coast. The village has retained most of its charm with many cobbled streets giving the feel of an old town and the houses draped with bougainvilleas of bright colours. Most of the houses tend to be single storey whilst they do not have a great deal of age due to most of the Algarve rebuild after the 1755 earthquake. Take a look at the chimneys as there are some elaborate ones known only to the Algarve. Chimneys were the signature of the builder, as well as a status symbol for the house owner. Porches have some good restaurants that mainly focus on evening dining; booking is advised in the summer months. Porches was known for its clay pits for hundreds of years and in the past produced the very large terracotta pots that you see dotted around. These were used for wine, water, and olive oil. There was a decline in pottery in the 19th century due to imports and modern techniques of cheaper and lighter pottery and china. These large pots can be seen in many places across the Algarve and have now become valuable antiques in their own right, selling for anything up to €2,000.

A revival in pottery came to the village in the late 1960s. A new pottery studio was founded, not by a Portuguese, but an Irish artist, Patrick Swift. Porches pottery has now become well known across Europe. It has a distinct quality, which is easily recognized, with decorative pieces in the Moorish tradition. It also produces everyday items that are intended for use in the home. The pottery studio has an open area where you can see the artist at work decorating the pottery. Outside is a café serving refreshments and light lunches. Just further down the road from Porches is Senhora da Rocha and its little chapel with parts dating from the 15th century. It has one of the most 'picture-postcard' coastal views of the Central Algarve.

The chapel hold a yearly festival taking the statue of Our Lady out to sea for a blessing ceremony for the fishermen. Below the beach is divided into two with a 100 metre-long tunnel joining the two beaches. On the eastern side is a small fisherman's beach with public toilets, showers and baby changing. There are two dedicated disabled parking places, with decking going down to the beach. Caution signs have been erected as the area is subject to cliff erosion, so care is needed when choosing your spot on the beach to spend the day.

Salir

Salir in the Central Algarve comes under the district of Loulé located along the EN124 that runs from the town of Alcoutim, near the Spanish border, to the medieval fortified town of Silves in the Central Algarve. Salir sits over 200 metres above sea level, set in the Serra de Caldeirao hills as the back drop. This can be seen when heading towards the castle ruin of Salir. The town seems to be divided into two halves due to dipping in the middle, with the main church (Igreja Matriz), which dates from the 16th century, on one high point, and the castle ruin dating from the 12th century on the other. If exploring the town with a young family caution is needed when using the footpath leading to the rear of the castle.

Whilst the path gives spectacular views across to the main church and the lush green hills of the Serras, it just has a high handrail of wooden posts with a single rope. You can just as easily venture through the small cobbled streets and reach the castle ruin that way: you could follow the cobbled pavement down the side of the small church, with its hand-carved stone cross that sits alone on a plinth.

The castle has no real significant splendour, unlike the huge castle of Silves.

It was thought Salir Castle was mainly to protect farm workers who worked the land, growing valuable food crops. Often there were attacks from Christian fighters who were seeking food sources for their fighting armies. The sight of any forte or castle would be a deterrent. Whilst the castle remains are small they are of significant importance to Portugal's history, as one of the few remaining ruins dating back to the Moors period.

Salir holds a medieval fair each year (Salir do Tempo) during September over a three-day period. Funding from the Loulé council assures a spectacular event. Everyone dressing in period Moorish costume makes it feel believable, especially when hearing music being on instruments styled from the period. There is a smaller fair held in the square in May (Corn

Festival). The square is behind the main church next to the large white water tower that dominates the town.

Salir is very well maintained. It seems strange to see the choice of large Victorian-style street lamps attached to the small single-storey cottage walls. But they do add charm to the town.

When wandering the small cobbled streets the main road circles the town. It has a good choice of smaller shops, cafés/bars and restaurants for those visiting Salir with lunch in mind. Salir, being inland, has no daily fish market so fresh fish is brought in daily from Loulé's large daily undercover market.

Nearby Fonte Benemola is a protected wildlife area offering some great walking routes. Easily spotted by the brown signs dotted around, the area is well known for its wildlife which includes the habitats of otters. The spring erupts in stunning colour from wild flowers native to this part of Portugal.

Sao Bartolomeu de Messines

Sao Bartolomeu de Messines sits in the Central Algarve under the district of Silves. Steeped in history, it offers much to explore, yet it is hard to come across in most tourist guides. Offering two free museums, it lends itself to having so much, due to the fact that the town sits in a basin and retains what other towns lost in the earthquake of 1755. Situated just off the EN124 towards Silves. With views of the whole town from the road, it beckons you to wander down, and explore what it has to offer.

The first building you will see, sitting in the town centre, is the church (Igreja Matriz). Not just another one of the Algarve's old churches, this is a marvel, originating from 16th century, with a style somewhere between Manueline and Renaissance, to which a baroque façade was added during the 18th century.

The elaborate front stone doorway has the date '1716' carved into it. The front of the church is rather impressive, with the contrast of white walls and red sandstone that is unique to the Silves area.

Even if religion is of no interest to you, the inside is well worth a visit. They have put wooden ramps for wheelchair access; if you have any difficulty the police station is just two doors away and a helping hand will always be on offer.

Opposite the church is a museum: the birthplace of the 19th century poet, João de Deus, whose book *Cartilha Maternal* was widely used to teach reading and writing during the late 19th and early 20th centuries. This museum is of interest to all ages and is open to the public with free entry. It is in two parts, showing the original house as it was when Joao de Deus lived there: even the original furniture features. It also offers an art gallery, with items collected from the 19th century onwards. It has left a legacy as it is still used today as a teaching place for small numbers of children, but has become more up-to-date, with computers.

The town has a large central undercover daily market with fresh fish, cured meats, breads, and fruit and vegetables. With many shops and bars and cafés, this is a town whose community supports itself, and even has its own football grounds.

Many backstreets show the wealth that the town once had, with its many merchants' houses with fancy wrought iron Juliet balconies and window shutters.

Most streets are single lane, with archways and courtyards giving the town the feeling of stepping back in time. By the main road near the church the older generation can often be seen playing dominoes and cards whilst sitting in the wooden shelter. There is a monthly market where all the smaller villages meet and buy pots and pans, clothing, plants, fruit and veg, smoked cheeses and cured meats.

Situated towards the outskirts of the town and easily seen when looking down upon entering the town from the Algoz end, there is a new building just near the exit towards Algoz and Lisbon. This is the other free museum, open Monday-Friday 9:30-13:00 & 14:00-17:30. There are exhibits of costumes through the ages and work tools and other items. They hold open air festivals with traditional games of the past: fun for all!

Other nearby places of interest is the Funcho dam. The views are spectacular, with hills all around looking down to the reservoir below. The only sounds heard are bees buzzing in the trees and an occasional cricket. It would be the perfect place to relax with a good book or picnic, away from any crowds.

Silves

Silves in central Algarve is a city steeped in history and would suit all tastes. The first thing you notice on the approach is the magnificent castle standing with its unique red rock known to the district, along with the main church sitting at the top, and the large city hall building. History takes Silves back to many ages, yet little is known about it before the Arab occupation. Silves has a population of around 11,000.

It beggars belief what the city must have been like in its heyday, when Silves was the capital back in the 15th Century. The build-up of silt to the main river halted trade, bringing it to a standstill. The river stayed that way until 2009 when work began to restore the river back to a working waterway, and now river trips are again possible. In summer months, it is well worth taking one of these trips up river towards Portimao.

Silves is easily a full day-trip, with so much to offer from the moment you enter the city: there are views of the old bridge spanning the river, with parkways further along towards Monchique. The large indoor daily market, found along the front, sells fresh fish, cheeses and cured meats, etc.

You can stroll through the many narrow streets with the bars and restaurants, along with the many shops mingled among them. The city has its resident storks that can be found nesting above your head in the many tall chimneys.

Further along are water features with marble statues depicting its history; here is where the medieval fair is held every year. You can partake and dress in 15th-century style costumes to get a feel for how it must have been. The fair offers jousting on horseback in an old-style fort arena, built each year for the occasion: well worth watching. The city has many stalls selling mostly Moroccan gifts, giving the spirit of the evening. It is one time a year which brings Silves alive, held over a ten-day period in August.

Whilst slowly making your way to the top, towards the castle, look out for the beautiful hand-painted tiles by local artist Kate Swift from the Swift family, part of the Porches Pottery. You will find museums in the backstreets including a Moroccan culture museum. Local craft shops dotted along the cobble streets look exactly as you would expect from a medieval city, but most that you see will be from post-1755 as the big earthquake that hit the whole of Portugal destroyed much of Silves, to the extent that it was abandoned for many years, except for the few with no option but to stay, who rebuilt the city to what you see today. If visiting the castle on a Sunday you will hear the local bistro with its live music throughout the year at Café Ingles. The castle, now restored after much excavation work, offers a good insight into the past history of Silves. Views across the city from the castle walls will make you realise what a beautiful place Silves really is. The large impressive building at the top is the council/planning offices.

Come midday, it is the time to relax at many of the traditional restaurants, with fresh fish always on the menus. The unmistakable smell of grilled fish and chicken fills the air with its aroma. This is when the city starts to buzz as the office workers come to enjoy a relaxing two-hour lunch break. Not to be missed is the flea market held near the waterfront every third Saturday of the month, offering items from furniture to small trinkets to take back home.

Tunes

Tunes in the Central Algarve comes under the district of Silves.

Many say that the village got its name from settlers from Tunis (Tunisia). The village was insignificant in the 1700s; it was not even mentioned on the William Faden maps of Portugal. (William Faden was a well-known map drawer of Europe.) Even in 1797, when nearby small villages of Algoz and Porches were included on maps, it was still overlooked.

Tunes came into its own in the 1890s when Portugal had the first railway in 1856 in Lisbon. The village has a coat of arms that has the steam train incorporated.

The need to expand to the far reaches of the Algarve was now seen as being important, due to the farming and mills in the area, as well as the fishing industry the Algarve was famous for, the warm Atlantic waters providing many varieties of different fish, especially tuna. It later produced a huge income for the Algarve, with tuna being one of the first fish canned in the 1900s.

The village today is divided in two by the railway line. This is four tracks wide with a direct link to Lisbon taking around four hours and running twice a day. Tunes went from slow diesel trains to the express electric trains in the year 2000. This is also one of very few trains that has dedicated wheelchair hoists, and dedicated disabled carriages.

The village has charm as one expects from the Algarve. The old metal water tower stands as a reminder that the town grew from the days of the steam train, when there was a need to fill trains with water at regular intervals to produce the steam.

Tunes has a good undercover daily market, for fresh fish and vegetables as well as daily baked bread. Found on the same side of the village is a monthly market held along the street on the fourth Saturday of the month, selling mainly shoes, clothes and household items. If travelling by car, head towards the A22 to reach the other side of the village. There are plenty of shops and a good choice of restaurants including a popular Indian restaurant. In 2013 the village merged its council with the village of Algoz. The main village hall is found in the centre of Algoz, giving any information needed about Tunes.

Quarteira

Quarteira in the Central Algarve comes under the district of Loulé: once just a small fishing village, but now a city, sitting between Vilamoura and Vale do Lobo. It seems to have concentrated too much at becoming a city with very wide roads that circle it, and many features on the roundabouts such as waterfalls and marble statues. The only signs of tourism are when heading towards the long sandy beach with its promenade, or the waterpark a few kilometres away on the outskirts, even though the city has grown over the years, with the many tall towering buildings.

When the infrastructure was put in they made the main high street wide with plenty of green space and a row of palms. The frontage has a long promenade, with half being pedestrian only. The promenade offers many parking bays, including dedicated disabled bays, with direct access to the beach, which is a long palm-lined one, with many water breaks to slow the tide, making swimming safer.

Toward the western side of the front sits a large blue and white building decorated with hand-painted tiles depicting scenes of Portuguese traditions. It's the daily indoor covered fresh fish and produce market, open until 1pm except Sundays.

Along the promenade front is the small tourist office located at the back of the large water fountain. This area offers free Wi-Fi, and is a favoured place for retired men sitting playing cards and dominoes. Next to the tourist office is a small museum with free entry. The theme is costumes and Quarteira's past; also along the front is a mobile library, open from 20th July to 31st August.

For those who holiday without car hire, Quarteira has a large bus station that will take you to most destinations across the Algarve. The town is suitable for families and groups of all ages due to being so flat; you can even walk along the waterfront to nearby neighbouring Vilamoura where you can book the many water sports on offer or boat/fishing trips. Near the Quarteira Camp site is the large weekly market held every Wednesday (see markets).

Quarteira has plenty to offer, with many bars, cafés and a good choice of restaurants. The area is well known for its green areas with the many stone pine trees. Use caution when picnicking near these trees as they can become home to large numbers of caterpillars that can give a nasty rash if touched. They are easy to spot as they leave web-like structures in the pine trees.

Vilamoura

Vilamoura, in the Central Algarve, is the name given to the area, rather than the town, which lacks its own period coat of arms. Vilamoura comes under the district of Loulé and is one of the richest districts in the Algarve, known for million euro villas and top golf courses. Vilamoura was created in the 1960s, built as one of the largest single tourist complexes in Europe, covering 1600 hectares of land. It is not known as the 'pine resorts' for nothing, with one of the largest pine tree covered areas in the Algarve. The high demand for luxury houses has led to the development and reclaim of the marshlands. The company that owns the complex is environmentally conscious and has made every effort to protect nature within its continued planned development.

Whilst Vilamoura comes across as an expensive place, due to the luxury boats and yachts moored in the marina that dominated the town and price tags for villas that can reach into the millions, yet you would be wrong for thinking it is not an affordable place to visit. There are plenty of restaurants to suit every pocket: try those bars and restaurants off the back road with a dish of the day from as little as €10.

For those of you who are golfers it offers six different golf courses (though the Championship course requires you to have a handicap certificate to play). The complex also includes a large marina, a lawn bowling club, a tennis club, a sports club, even a shooting club. There are 5-star and 4-star hotels, many apartments, self-catering villas and nightclubs. It also boasts a cinema and an excellent horseriding school.

Within the centre of Vilamoura is a preserved Roman site and the Museum of Cerro da Vila, providing a glimpse into the past of the area. The entrance fees are just €5 (as of 2014).

In Roman times this location was important in producing a fish paste known as garum. The ruins also include the baths in which the mariners used to bathe. The museum has both indoor and outdoor exhibits.

Vilamoura marina is the heart of the town, with a large range of restaurants, bars and shops (including many designer shops). The marina offers a chance to stroll and looks very picturesque in the evenings, with the 1000 berths nearly always full and the soft clang of the yachts' rigging as waves gently rock the boats.

The resort is also home to Vilamoura Casino, which has regular evening entertainment, such as dance and singing shows, separate from the gaming rooms.

It is well worth paying a visit to the main borough city of Loulé which is very café cultured and known for its two large markets (see Market dates).

Eastern Algarve

Alcoutim

Alcoutim in the Eastern Algarve is the most northerly point bordering the Alentejo region.

Alcoutim town is one of the Algarve's inland hidden gems, located along the Guadina River that faces Spain. The town is not very large, so it is well worth taking one of the parking spaces that are clearly marked along the roadside. There is also parking right on the riverfront, but these spaces are soon filled in the summer months. The town has much to offer and is steeped in history for those who are looking for adventure. The 13th-century castle, open to the public, offers spectacular views from the crenellation walls looking across the river to the Spanish town of Sanlucar de Guadiana, with its large white fort sitting on top of the hillside. The castle entrance fee is around €2.50: it is ideal for young families, as safety rails have been put in place on the parapet wall.

Many of Alcoutim's narrow cobbled streets are formed from stones taken from the riverbed, adding charm to the feel of the place. Alcoutim has retained many of the old walls dating from the 17th century when it was a garrison town, having four churches/chapels and an early customs house. The main square has a modern look: new granite cobbles make up the road that leads to the waterfront, where the road and parking area are laid with rock slate local to the area, as far as the slipway for launching boats. There you will also find public toilets. The waterfront, with weeping willow trees, offers shelter with stone benches to sit on and take in the view of the various boats that come and moor for a week or two. Moorings are based on a first-come basis, with charges doubling after the first week's stay. On the left side of the waterfront are beautiful public gardens and benches along with exercise seesaws, wheels and bikes that are a fixed feature of the gardens. Along the front is also a company which offers river boat trips and kayaking, cycle hire and minibus excursions to Spain. Those who are looking for a more daring adventure can zip-wire from Spain across to Alcoutim. Launched in 2013 as one of the first zip line rides to travel between two countries, this costs around €15 which includes the boat ferry crossing. There is a minimum age restriction of 14 years to use the ride.

Heading back into town, you come across marble statues depicting people along with colourful bougainvilleas climbing the church walls. Alcoutim has a small tourist office, banks, and pharmacy, plenty of small shops as well as handmade traditional crafts and ceramics.

There are plenty of bars/cafés, restaurants to sit in and enjoy the views of the boats sailing by with the backdrop of the San Carlos Castle and the silhouette of the stonework of La Iglesia de Nuestra Senora de las Flores (Church of Our Lady of Flowers), with its three bells.

Alcoutim is flanked by two rivers: one is the main Rio Guadiane and the other is Riberira de Cadavias. This smaller river divided Alcoutim which is now joined by two bridges. Over the other side is a day centre used by the elderly residents and a large school; further along is an arts centre with different displays. Further is a private kayak training centre. The road is a dead end and at one time had the Hotel Guadiana River, but that has since closed down. Alcoutim holds a five-day music festival in September.

Those wishing to visit by public transport can do so by bus from the town of Vila Real St Antonio.

Castro Marim

Castro Marim in the Eastern Algarve is the last town on the eastern side on the border with Spain, with the Guadiana River separating the two countries.

On approaching Castro Marim the town already has much to offer, with the castle beckoning you to explore. There is much history in the town, including an association with the Knights Templar, the guardians of the relics of the Protectors of Christ. Castro Marim has a large monthly market held on the second Saturday of the month. This is well worth the visit, offering a wide range from fresh fruit and vegetables to cheeses, hams, and local honey. There is an antiques market on the same day held just up the road in Vila real St Antonio (see Market dates). Heading towards Castro Marim from the west towards Spain, there is a strange array of five tall pillars with a windmill sitting above, as well as a chapel on the right-hand side. The tall pillars are water fountains, which only becomes clear when heading up towards the windmill.

There is a cultural centre with a small auditorium used when holding music and other events. The windmill is part of the museum: this is worth going up just for the spectacular views across to Spain with the riverside town of Ayamonte. There are salt beds that Portugal is known for; further along are marshes and wildlife conservation.

The main attraction for Castro Marim might well be the castle, now just a ruin, dating from the 9th Century. It is open to the public with plenty to see inside: displays of stocks and a small chapel, as well as other attractions. The entrance fee was just €1 in 2014; it is only possible to access by those who are strong walkers and is not suitable for the elderly or disabled due to the uneven approach road. But with the Fort of Sao Sebastiao dating from the 17th Century, on the other side of the town, offers better access for most. The best time to feel how the town must have been is when Castro Marim holds its annual medieval festival in August. The town comes to life for almost a week, re-enacting the Moorish period with everyone in costumes, music, dancing, sword skills, even a working blacksmith's. Castro Marim is quite flat with traditional cobblestone streets and pavements; this can be bumpy for wheelchair/pushchair users. It has a daily covered market and plenty of good restaurants. Note: for those dining out in the warmer evenings, the nearby marshes the town gets infested with mosquitoes at certain times of the year. It is easy to find the centre of town, with the large white church with a White House-style dome crowning the top. There are many small narrow cobbled streets with whitewashed-single storey houses.

The town lacks grander merchants' houses, due to Castro Marim having been a fortified town: for many years the threat of attacks was high.

Estoi

Estoi in the Eastern Algarve borders on the Central and Western Algarve in the Serra do Caldeirao foot hills. The town has much to offer and is well worth the inland trip. Estoi comes under the parish of Faro, famous for its palace (nicknamed the Pink Palace); more about this further down. When entering Estoi from the east, a Roman ruin stands, known as Milreu Roman ruins. The oldest part of the ruins is a 1st- or 2nd-century AD Roman villa, part of an agricultural settlement. Later, in the 3rd century AD, it was a luxurious house with a large bathing complex. Later it became a sanctuary, up until the 6th Century.

At the centre of Estoi sits an impressive church, with a mixture of styles: Corinthian columns for the entrance, with front façade of Roman influence, then a Moorish-style bell tower. At the bottom of the stone steps leading to the church entrance there is a running spring with three stone pipes leading into a solid stone trough.

A similar one is opposite with a tiled information plaque. Off the small square are bars and restaurants which lead to a cobbled street. At the end sits an impressive arched gateway that is part of the palace boundary. Estoi has many fine merchants' houses with carved stone adorning doorways and window surrounds, with fancy cast iron Juliet balconies. Estoi has other small squares in the town, with the influence of the Moorish period displayed in many of the larger houses. In the centre of the village is a daily indoor fish and fruit and vegetables market that is open until midday. Estoi is not just well known for its palace, holding huge events just off a side road from the main church. In May and August Estoi holds large equestrian shows that take place until the early hours. The parade has decorated horse-drawn carriages and buggies. The town gets a medieval feel as the fair is alight with flame torches. In the past there has also been bullfighting, but these are becoming less due to the animal rights that seem to be creeping in across Europe. On the same site is a large monthly market. The car park has dedicated parking for campervans (motorhomes).

The 'palace' was built at the end of the 18th century by a local aristocrat from the Carvalhal family. It is considered a fine example of neo-classical architecture; its interior has more of a French and Italian feel, with paintings of cherubs on walls and ceilings and furniture of the Louis XVI style. Estoi Palace remained in the Carvalhal family until 1893, when it was sold to a wealthy chemist and landowner from Central Portugal. The new owner had the palace restored and augmented by Portugal's pre-eminent architect of the time. He did such a good job that it earned the owner the title of Viscount of Estoi in 1906. The palace passed down through the family until falling into disrepair. In 1987 it was purchased by the Municipal Council of Faro.

Now a luxury hotel, it is free to walk around the palace and gardens even if not a staying guest. It is a good place to have a coffee or light lunch whilst taking in the splendor of the former palace. On the exit road around the outer walls of the palace gardens is the town's public laundry, its tiled covered roof now restored and wall decorated with hand painted tiles depicting its former use.

Faro City

Faro is the Algarve's biggest city and has the main airport for the Algarve. Whilst not so well known as a holiday destination, Faro can be a good base for any holiday. (London is not seen primarily as a holiday destination, but still attracts millions every year.)

Faro has its fair share of history and culture, along with places of interest. With a population close to 70,000 it has become the capital of the Algarve. The city of Silves lost popularity as the main city of the Algarve, due to the decline in trade when river silt caused the river to become difficult to navigate. Faro is the main administrative centre for the whole of the Algarve region. Faro has both Arab and Roman ruins, but most of the present older buildings were constructed after the disastrous earthquake of 1755. Many have old wrought iron balconies and parapet walls with statues and urns. The Moors who occupied the town in the 8th Century originally gave it the name of Ossonoba, then developed it into a trading port until 1249, when they were defeated by the forces of Dom Afonso III.

Hand-painted tiles in the various public buildings depict scenes from this major battle in the history of Portugal. Similar tiles can be seen on the benches in Portimao in the main square near the fountain.

Faro has a Cathedral as well as many churches with the finest hand-carved wooden altar backdrops, lavishly decorated in 24ct gold leaf. But the most famous is the city's 'golden' church of *Nossa Senhora do Carmo*, the best example of such decoration in southern Portugal. It also contains the macabre chapel lined with the bones from over 1,200 monks.

Particularly attractive is the old part of the city surrounded by the Roman walls that were rebuilt by the moors in the 9th century. Inside is a spacious open square that was once the site of the Roman forum. A 13th-century Cathedral faces the 18th-century Episcopal palace. Another nearby building worth a visit is the 16th-century convent, now the home of the city's archaeological museum, covering the period of the Moorish occupation.

Next to the small harbour/marina bordering the *Praça de Dom Francisco Gomes* is the small naval museum, displaying intricate detailed scale-model ships, boats and galleons, showing the maritime history of the navy and a sailor's working life in Portugal.

There is also the Faro Jewish Heritage Centre, which consists of a cemetery and a small museum. It still has strong active connections today. Much of Faro is now a thriving scene with everyday shops, restaurants and nightclubs to cater for those who live in the city centre. Faro is also the home of the *Ria Formosa* lagoon nature reserve. Over 17,000 hectares in area, this is a stopping place for hundreds of different species of birds, arriving in the spring mating season, then migrating in autumn period.

The beach is a bit of a trek, being 7 kilometres distant from the city. A long sandy beach reached by crossing a wooden bridge, it is not far from the airport. Faro holds many annual events and fairs and it is well worth contacting the tourist office to see what's on during your visit.

Fuzeta

Fuzeta in the Eastern Algarve comes under the district of the nearby town of Olhao. You will often find two types of spelling for this town: Fuzeta or Fuseta. Both are correct, having been derived from the old spelling Fozeta (the word 'foz' meaning mouth, used in the term 'mouth of the river'). Fuzeta sits on the estuary that joins to the Atlantic Ocean.

Fuzeta is a thriving fishing town and due to the warmer waters still has large catches of tuna. This forms part of the canning industry that the Algarve is known for. Fuzeta is also a large producer of natural sea salt from the salt beds that lie to the eastern side of the town. Campers and motorhomes are in for a treat as Fuzeta campsite is situated by the quayside, with views across the small islands that give Fuzeta its beach. This is accessible by taking the ferry to Armona-Fuseta.

If visiting the islands you have a choice of the water taxi which can be more expensive than the ferry. The difference is that the taxi leaves when you want, while the ferry leaves at certain intervals.

Fuzeta is laid out like a grid; the many small streets as well as the main one criss-cross each other. It has much to offer, with a main decorated cobbled pedestrian street with shops, bars and art gallery that leads to a small square, with trees that offer shade and public benches. The square is flanked on each side with many bars and restaurants for those who want to soak up the atmosphere the town offers. Many roads are either no entry, or one way.

To be honest there's no real reason to want to drive around the narrow streets, as you would miss the real Fuzeta. There are many buildings that will have you reaching for the camera, from traditionally tiled to those with glazed balustrade decorating parapet walls. Some even have heart-shaped panels in the windows.

Most have hand-carved stone window and door surrounds that you no longer see in today's building. If you venture down you will come across the main church square, with the Chapel of our Lady of Carmo. Like many fishing towns in the Algarve Fuzeta is no exception when it comes to the religious precessions that take place each year.

One statue of "Our Lady" is placed on a fishing boat then taken out to sea, as part of the blessing for the fishermen's safety: quite a breathtaking event, with many fishing boats decorated in palm leaves and flowers as part of the ceremony, to which all are welcome. Fuzeta has a good-sized daily fresh fish market down by the harbour, as well as a street market every Thursday, and an antique/flea market held monthly. Buyers and sellers come from as far as Spain.

You can easily spend the whole day investigating what Fuzeta has to offer. During the winter months it becomes very popular with tourists who use the park open area to play the traditional game of boule (similar to bowls but using steel bowls).

The Algarve has recently encouraged walking and cycling along the many walking and cycle routes as part of its promotion of the Eco-way for Europe. For those wishing to stay or camp in the town it offers good public transport links, with bus and trains to further your adventure of Portugal.

Moncarapacho

Moncarapacho in the Eastern Algarve comes under the district of Olhao that gained city status in 1985 due to the importance of its tourist centre.

Moncarapacho might not be something tourists would expect to visit since it is known more for being an agricultural area. But you would be missing a part of the Algarve that is well worth the visit.

There is a museum (Museu Paroquial) housing artefacts from all periods, with a good display just outside in the enclosed courtyard, ranging from Roman pillars and carved marble finials to pre-Roman stone drinking troughs. It does seem strange to see such an impressive collection in the middle of a small village. But this is due to the area's agricultural use: most have been discovered when ploughing land to plant crops and trees in the surrounding areas.

This element of the town is celebrated with a very large agriculture-themed market/event in August and is attended by locals from surrounding villages. It continues with live music and food festivals into the small hours. It is not just for locals: all are welcome to join in the fun.

The town has some very unusual architecture, one being the Moorish façade of the GNR building (police station) and another the elaborate stone-carved doorway of the main church, dating back to the 18th century. There is also a smaller chapel (Santo Cristo) next door to the museum that has a bell tower and dates from 1704.

Most of the streets and pavements are the traditional cobblestones which give the town its unique charm. Many typically Algarvian houses are single storey with decorative parapet walls and grand chimneys. The more lavish two-storey houses with their Juliet balconies are more likely to have been trade merchants' houses.

The main square is planted with palms and flowering trees; cafés and bars with tables and chairs on their terraces in the warmer weather offer welcomed shade from the trees. Moncarapacho has plenty of small mini-markets, bakers, butchers and a monthly street market selling fresh fruit and vegetables, cheeses, hams and breads.

There are a few restaurants that give a varied choice of traditional Portuguese cuisine as well as homemade traditional wood fire oven-baked pizzas. If you are staying in the town and want fresh fish to cook, the nearby quayside town of Fuzeta is just 8 kilometres away. It has a ferry that will take you to the islands' beaches for a few euros per person. You will find it is easy to reach most towns and places of interest by either the motorway (toll fees apply) or the nearby EN125 toll-free road.

Monte Gordo

Monte Gordo in the Eastern Algarve is a large spacious town, with many streets dedicated to pedestrians. There is a good feel of space that surrounds the town, due to the fact the streets are very wide. It is just a few kilometres from the furthest eastern town in the Algarve, Vila real St Antonio, which sits on the Spanish border.

The two towns are so different in so many ways. Monte Gordo has the Casino Hotel, which opened in the late 1990s, bringing big changes to the town with many the high-rises that soon followed. Monte Gordo has a long and wide golden beach with no buildings built on the beach side to ruin the coastline view of the town. Monte Gordo sees much traffic, with people flocking to the hugely popular beach. Portable toilets are laid on in the car parks during peak season to cope with the influx of tourists in the summer. The town has a well laid out park close to the beach front, which gets popular with Portuguese families taking a picnic, offering plenty of seating in the shade when hot summer months prevail.

Monte Gordo has many good Portuguese restaurants, along with the feel of being a traditional town rather one catering for tourists, like the popular town of Albufeira in the Central Algarve. There is ample parking with a pay-to-park very near the beach along the palm-lined promenade. Monte Gordo holds a monthly antiques market on the fourth Saturday of every month.

The main beach of Monte Gordo stretches for miles. It has the benefit of being close to the Spanish border, with the Mediterranean waters creeping in, giving higher water temperatures. The beach has many long lengths of beach decking running along and down, providing good access for pushchairs and disabled people. Monte Gordo´s road structure is easy to use with one-way and no-entry streets clearly marked. Those looking for gift shops should head for the signposted 'pedonol' (pedestrian) zone, making shopping with younger children less stressful due to no-traffic-allowed roads.

Olhao

Olhao is a coastal town on the Eastern Algarve: on arrival it may not seem appealing, but don't let that fool you. The town has as much to offer as any other. Olhao enjoys a marina; it has no beach to call its own, but further along you can catch the ferry to *Ria Formosa* lagoon. The ferries for the ilhas beach run from the quayside near the gardens, at the eastern end of the red brick market buildings.

There are regular services during the peak season, with fewer crossings during the winter months. Olhao is more of an exploring town rather than one filled with tourist attractions, although down by the waterfront you will find a small pleasant park strip, offering shaded seating areas in the summer months. It also has a children's play area with safety flooring.

The large red brick buildings architecturally look in keeping with their Moorish-style dome towers. But the red brick itself seems out of place for the Algarve. They house the daily market place, which consists of two identical buildings. Once inside the market offers an array of fresh fish, fruit and vegetables, with its cafés that run along the outside terraces. Even if not planning to buy anything, it is well worth exploring. As catches are brought in daily by the fishermen, it will have many varieties you will have never seen.

Outside, its surrounding bars and cafés make a pleasant place to sit and take in the busy waterside atmosphere. With plenty of waterfront parking, this is an ideal spot to start a touring the town, as most of the rest of the town is pay and display parking: when looking around, time can soon pass, and dashing back to top up parking fees can be a headache. Heading toward the centre through the many backstreets, you find houses with their Juliet cast-iron balconies and stone surrounds door and window surrounds, often owned by trading merchants who showed off their wealth on the outside of their houses. You get a feel of days gone by, with the streets remaining unchanged for over 250 years. In the main square, you cannot help notice the huge church of Nossa Senhora do Rosário, built in 1698 with contributions from the fishermen when it was the first stone building in Olhao. Remarkably, it survived the 1755 earthquake, standing as a proud and beautiful building with its history known to the locals, but its façade was built to impress father than fit in with its surroundings. The town has a museum and can be identified by its statue of our lady standing in a niche right above the door. The town offers a good assortment of shops and many restaurants, with the main theme being locally caught fish. Not to be missed in August is the Olhao seafood festival, one of the largest of its kind in the Algarve, attracting around 50,000 visitors during the festival period.

Pechao

Pechao in the Eastern Algarve falls under the parish of Olhao, being a main fishing town just 5 kilometres away. Being so close to Olhao makes it well worth a visit, with the main church that sits on the highest point offering stunning coastal views. One of the few towns or villages in the Algarve that also has a bone chapel, Pechao's is a bone chapel with a difference: it is an open monument. It was planned that a small chapel would be built, but instead the main flank wall to the main entrance was all that remained, with skulls and bones set into the wall.

Just beside the church you will also see a museum and combined art gallery, open on Wednesday to Sunday 4pm - 7pm. The museum houses varied antique agriculture-related items and sewing crafts traditional to the area.

As with most inland villages, figs, olives, and almonds are a thriving and important part of the economy. Other places of interest are the Old Fountain, the Museum of Pechao, and Chalet Belamandil.

There is much that goes on in Pechao throughout the year. In March it holds a large marathon; in 2012 it held the seventh event, named March Athletica de Pechao, with up to 500-600 taking part and onlookers cheering at the finish line.

Other big events include the three-day motorcycle event held in June (Motto Pechao) and the nearby Rock na Ribeira. This is an ideal event for the younger generation with many well-known bands performing. One great festival that Pechao is known for is held on the 25th of April, which is a public holiday (Liberty Day): Festival do Folar (festival of folklore) with street parades where hundreds of balloons in the Portuguese colours (green, red and yellow) are released into the sky, with music and dancing held just on the outskirts at the football pitches, along with many stalls selling the traditional Easter cinnamon spice cake.

Back in the 1590s Pechao came under the district of Faro, but along with nearby Olhao, its fishing fleets soon saw a huge growth and an increased importance to the fishing trade and canning industry. The large stone church, built in 1698 with contributions from the fishermen, sits proudly overlooking Pechao. The town began to gain such importance that Olhao took Pechao into its parish in the 1820s.

Today Pechao has a couple of minimarkets, a pharmacy, and a good choice of restaurants and numerous bars and cafés; even though Pechao is inland, it is close enough to Olhao for the local restaurants to serve fresh fish of the day.

Pechao is about 25 minutes from Faro airport, making it an ideal place to have lunch and wander around if you need to fill time before your flight.

Quelfes

Quelfes in the Eastern Algarve is a small village within the District of Olhao situated on the EN398 road between Olhao and Moncarapacho. For those using Google maps, the road will not show as the EN398. The village has swelled in the number of its residents, which has doubled in the past 20 years to 20,000.

Quelfes has made a name for itself as one of the large monthly market places to visit, holding an antiques market on the fourth Sunday of the month, with buyers coming from as far afield as Spain. The monthly local produce market held on the 5th Sunday, with locals coming from surrounding villages. Both markets are well worth visiting and are arranged in an orderly fashion within a large purpose-laid-out market square, consisting of hard-standing tarmac (so no muddy shoes should it rain). The square is easily found just 50 metres from the main church of the town on the main road. Quelfes also has a small village hall/tourist office. The main church (Igreja Matriz de Quelfes) dates from the 16th century. Quelfes' coat of arms has a bridge which might appear insignificant to many visitors. For those seeking history, it refers to the restored Roman bridge just before you reach Quelfes coming from Olhao: undergoing restoration over many years and spanning nearly 27 metres in length, this was also a place where Napoleon's troops were defeated back in 1808.

Quelfes does not offer any tourist attractions other than the market. The village is basically set alongside the main road. On the side of the road are two old Noras (water wells) that have a large wheel used draw up water when turned by hand. The village holds religious festivals, one being the feast of St Sebastian held at the end of January. The other is a larger one held over two days in June and well celebrated by the locals. There are a couple of bars where you can stop off for coffee or beer.

Santa Barbara de Nexe and Bordeira

Santa Barbara de Nexe, on the border of Central and Eastern Algarve, is in the district of Faro, the largest City in the Algarve. The main centre of the village is the church, which sits on higher ground from the main high street; the bell tower, said to date from the 18th century, is a local landmark that can be seen for miles. There is a small garden square which offers shaded seating areas. The village is popular with English and Dutch people who have settled in the village; a well-known celebrity from the rock group Iron Maiden has a house nearby. The village has a local school, plenty of small shops, an ATM cash machine, and a new large supermarket and garage on the outer edge of the village.

In August, Portugal has a public holiday on the 15th; this is celebrated throughout the country, as it is Assumption, a religious holiday. The village of Santa Barbara de Nexe is no exception and hosts a celebration in the main high street, with stage acts. The village has no monthly market, with the nearest being held in nearby Estoi, the second largest in the Algarve.

Bordeira

Just a few kilometers away is the smaller village of Bordeira which shares its name with another village in the Western Algarve. Bordeira is more or less a main street, with several restaurants and a small antiques shop mainly selling farm implements and iron beds. The village has no church, nor anything to offer tourists who are sightseeing, other than the general charm of the Algarve. There is an old Nora which was used communally to draw up water; this is now no longer in use. However, the area is popular with holiday renters, who flock to the large restaurant in the village: it is well known for traditional cuisine, which also makes it popular with the locals.

Sao Bras de Alportel

Sao Bras de Alportel in the Eastern Algarve nestles inland. The town, with all its charm and character, could easily be missed if you just stick to visiting coastal towns. The first thing you notice is how much cooler it is than other places, due to its high position, which also gives sea views to the coast. Once a Roman settlement, with the old part of the town still retaining many narrow streets, Sao Bras de Alportel is a town for all ages, and you can easy spend the whole day exploring what it has to offer. When you approach the town you come across a Lidl supermarket with modern buildings surrounding it, but go across the roundabout and all is revealed.

When you come into the old part of town just off the side street, there are lavish merchants' houses with their hand-painted tiled frontages with fancy cast iron Juliet balconies and statues sitting on parapet walls. The unusual twin-tower church has two clocks, one on each bell tower. The town has many tiny backstreets that are well worth venturing down, with plenty of fascinating finds. There is a cultural information office, with much information on the town and history, with displays of local produced including lace work. It often holds events in the well-kept gardens with views over the public swimming baths. There is a tourist office further into the town. The main square in the town offers ample parking with many coffee/bars in the surrounding area. One of the town's largest churches is well worth a visit, as is the museum on the corner of Rua 1° De Maio and Rua Dr. Jose Rosa Da Silva.

In the 17th century the town was known for its coolness compared to the coast; it was favoured by the bishops across the Algarve and Portugal. The church had a palace built for them to use during the hot summer months; now it has other uses. Although the wealth of the town declined, due to the large cork production being moved further inland into central Portugal, Sao Bras de Alportel is still a busy place, and whilst popular with tourists it still has a thriving Portuguese population along with local traditions, with markets selling many local products.

St Catarina

Santa (St) Catarina in the Eastern Algarve comes under the district of Tavira. It is situated along the EN270 road which runs from Tavira in the East to just past Loulé in the Central Algarve. The Coat of Arms shows a wheel with razors: this is known as the Catherine Wheel, associated with St Catherine of Alexandria.

On approaching the village from the east you cannot help but notice the large ugly factory building with the Cooperative Agricultural building next door. There are four granite cone-shaped stones used to grind grain and olives. The area plays an important role for locals in the pressing of olives into oil. Normally ten kilos of olives gives the grower one litre of first pressed olive oil. Alternatively they can sell the olives direct. When the factory is open you can go in and see the displays they have which explain the whole process. It is fascinating to see the old machinery on display with plaques (in English) that explain how the olive oil is produced.

Ask most people in the Algarve and they will know that St Catarina is well known for its handmade terracotta tiles that you find on many villa floors. They are sought after by those wishing to put character into a building. They have tried to mass-produce them in a modern way but you can easily tell the difference. Stacked by hand when dry then fired in old open oven Kilns. Whilst they are known as St Catarina tiles, most are made outside the village, but in surrounding areas.

St Catarina is mainly made up of the main high street, which has a bank with an ATM machine, chemist, post office and local newsagents, who sell English and German newspapers, due to the nearby camping site.

There is a mini supermarket and about four café/bars that offer a light lunch. Just off the main high street is the small square in which stands the impressive church with its clock and bell tower that rings out to surrounding areas.

Parts of the church date back to the 16th century. Some back roads are one-way; you can easy make a mistake by driving the wrong way due to the lack of signs.

The village has a good-sized monthly market dating back to 1814, selling fruit and veg, cheeses, hams and fresh local olives as well as poultry and farming tools. It is a mass meeting place for the locals from the surrounding hamlets.

St Catarina has a main church: it goes without saying that it also enjoys the religious celebrations, and food festivals that go with it, some lasting three days. There are spectacular displays, with a statue of Our Lady paraded along the streets with fresh flowers surrounding the statues carried by locals high on their shoulders. Fairs are on May Day, the feast of our Lady of Sorrows held in August and the feast of Patron on 25th November. Just outside the village at Fonte do Bispo is a carvery restaurant that is popular – even more so for holding a small flea market on the fourth Sunday of the month.

Tavira

Tavira, set in the Eastern Algarve towards the Spanish border, has to be the jewel in the crown of the Algarve. It has all that a picture-postcard town should have, and more. Taviras' status is a city, but it continues to be a lively fishing place with many of its roads still cobbled. Even the pavements are decorated with hand-laid black and white square cobbles with traditional designs. The city has a Roman bridge with seven arches that span the river Gilao, now only open to pedestrians due to flooding in the late 1980s. But it is not all bad as this means you can stand on the bridge with peace of mind, taking in the view and the marvellous architecture on both sides of the river. You might even catch a glimpse, when the tide is out, of fishermen wading in the mud looking for clams and other shellfish. It has palm trees on one side, where there is a small parkland strip with bandstand and gardens. This makes a welcome spot to sit in the summer months under the shade of the trees. This beautiful city can capture your interest all day, so making plans for lunch should be on the agenda. You can see from the wealth of the buildings that it must have been an important trading port in the 17th and 18th centuries.

Tavira has the remains of a castle which like most of Portugal was destroyed by the huge earthquake of 1755.

The old market hall on the river has undergone restoration and now houses shops, bars/cafes and restaurants, making an ideal break stop. Look for events held in the centre too. In addition the market hall makes an ideal meeting place: trying to meet up at one of the churches could prove a big mistake as Tavira has 37. Even the 16th-century Igreja da Misericórdia, seen as one of the finest in Eastern Algarve, is found near the tourist office. Wandering down the many backstreets, you will find many town houses with their tiled fronts and wrought iron Juliet balconies. With many lines of washing hanging out, it gives a feeling of being in a different time.

It is best to take your time at a pace that suits, exploring the city with its stunning buildings. Often when following a guide book you tend to dash from one listing to another, missing the real sense of the everyday life that goes on in ancient cities, with backstreets getting forgotten. The beach at Tavira is a fabulous island beach (Ilha de Tavira). Over 10 kilometres long, it accessed by ferry crossings from the city centre throughout the summer. All year round at nearby Quatro Aguas you will also notice the salt pans with piles of white salt crystals that are harvested in the season. For those interested in architectural heritage of the Tavira, the council has produced a booklet about recent archaeological discoveries in Tavira, covering defensive structures of the Phoenician, Islamic and Portuguese periods along with a guide to their location. The book can be obtained from the tourist office: it is called *The Military Architectural Heritage of Tavira*.

NOTE: Tavira parking is pay and display on most streets. If you are planning to visit for a day trip then finding parking on the outskirts would be the better choice.

A shopping centre on the outskirts is the Gran-Plaza shopping mall with a good choice of shops, places to eat and cinemas as well as a large Continente supermarket.

Vila Real de Santo Antonio

Vila Real de Santo Antonio is in the Eastern Algarve, situated on the far northwest tip of Portugal. The city lies on the Guadiana river bordering Spain, with the river flowing into the Atlantic Ocean. It has views of the city of Ayamonte on the Spanish side.

Vila Real has always had a history of fishing which over the years has declined; the new marina built in 1998 now houses many luxury boats. It is very popular, being so close to the Mediterranean Sea with its easy access to the rest of Europe. The riverfront is often the point where many fairs are held; typical is the monthly antiques market with buyers and dealers flocking over the Spanish border to snap up a bargain. The market is normally held in the main square, but more often than not many craft and other fairs use the square. If you want to go to Spain by ferry you can go to a building on the Avenida da Republica, once used for customs control, and buy ferry tickets for crossing to Ayamonte in Spain or going on various river tours. It is easy to recognise, with beautiful hand-painted tiles along the kilometre-long riverside promenade, which is attractively laid out with trees and water features. There is also a marina where you can watch the boats. Part of the Avenida da Republica runs alongside the Rio Guadiana at the front of the city, with evidence that Vila Real once had wealth in the elaborately designed buildings, some of which were grand hotels in their day. On entering the main square you can't help but notice the huge stone obelisk which is a monument to King Jose I and was unveiled to the town in 1775, just 20 years after the earthquake of 1755 which destroyed so much of Portugal. The main square, having seen much renovation to its surrounding buildings and with many orange trees, is a great place to sit and watch the world go by in one of the many bars and restaurants. Moving out of the square, the shops are plentiful with a wide range of goods; amongst the shops is the old market building which is often open for many different exhibitions and events. There are also museums to look out for. One is Museu de Manuel Cabanas: this houses wood engravings and paintings by a modern-day artist.

The new market is now three times the size of its predecessor and is under cover. It has a good deal of fresh produce, with fresh tuna at around €10 a kilo – great for the BBQ – as well as varieties of fish the average person has never seen before. Don't be afraid to try something different. (See the food/drink page for fish translations.) When travelling in the evening you cannot help but notice the lighthouse built around the 1920s: it stands 40 feet tall. Today it is automated, needing no lighthouse keeper.

Western Algarve

Aljezur

Aljezur is in the Western Algarve. When you approach Aljezur from the east on the N120 road, the first thing you notice is the long high street, which continues over the bridge to the other half of the town. Aljezur is in two parts, separated by the river. This came about in the mid-18th century due to the local bishop who was convinced that moving the town across the river would end the malaria the town suffered, with many daily deaths occurring. The people who stayed in the old part of town more than likely would not have been able to afford the cost of moving across the river. At one point on the left-hand side of the bridge is a small daily undercover market where fresh fish is plentiful. You will find a tourist office situated in the high street, with a free map of the town and other literature for the castle.

Before you dismiss the old part of the town and venture to the new part, you will find before the bridge a hostel that is popular with young backpackers. Continuing past this you will come across many cobblestone streets that head up hill. It is well worth venturing up to the top for the breathtaking views over the new town. There is a museum. For those who like to hike you can walk up to the castle ruin, which offers free admission. If you prefer to drive up to the ruin, you can do so quite easily. You will find many bars and restaurants in the old part where you can have coffee or lunch before venturing to the new part of the town across the river. Just before the bridge is the daily covered fish market. Open until 1pm and closed on Sundays, it has public toilets to the side of the market. On the short walk across the bridge to the second half of the town, you have the view of the main church ahead, with the green hills that surround Aljezur.

Due to the fact that this is very much farming country, with many small strips of land which are often shared by families that work the land, it is well worth making your way to the main church as you are rewarded with spectacular views. A couple of bars give an opportunity for a well-deserved break. The church square has a life of its own with locals sitting and chatting as the trees offer good shade in the hot summer months.

Alvor

Alvor on the Western side of the Algarve was once just a small fishing village, a hidden gem that few had heard about. Nowadays Alvor has become one of the favourites with tourists, still keeping its charm and remaining unspoilt. Any new buildings which increase the size of Alvor must be kept to minimum height, so as not to blot the landscape. No amount of building can take away the original unspoilt cobblestone roads that lead down to the harbour. If you want to buy fresh fish it can be possible to do so direct from the fishermen as they pull the boats in down by the lifeboat station. The waterfront is the main attraction as the River Rio joins there, getting the best of both worlds: the bay and the marina. EU funding was spent on bringing the Algarve up to modern-day standards, including disabled access to most places, with much of Alvor seeing these improvements, even down to the new fishing huts where fishermen can often be seen repairing their nets. The palm tree-lined walkway, with restaurants and bars, is the perfect place to enjoy the fresh barbecued fish while soaking up the atmosphere. Further along is the golden sandy beach with small coves; be aware of the new warning signs as many parts of the Algarve saw rock falls in 2010, with fatalities. Most famously noted is the earthquake of 1755 which destroyed much of Portugal.

Alvor has kept its layout with backstreet lanes having many low roof houses, some with decorated parapet walls.

The town attracted many cultures; its many restaurants reflect this. Eating out here has something for everyone; even bars vary from English and Irish to traditional Portuguese. Yet despite this, Alvor does not have an uncomfortable feel of a tourist resort, but more of a relaxed atmosphere. Sitting out in the warm evenings is something everybody enjoys whilst on holiday. During the day all that changes, with a good choice of mini supermarkets and fresh produce shopping and coffee breaks being on most people's minds. Come lunchtime the smell of the barbecues fill the air. There is still plenty of history and old buildings you can seek out, like the Igreia Matriz, dating from the 16th Century: its hand-carved stonework shows off its doorways and arches. The original 16th-century parish church, rebuilt after the earthquake of 1755, is still a prime example of great craftsmanship of the Manueline era of architecture. It was the only important building in Alvor that survived the earthquake. History shows that in 1495 King Joao II died in Alvor after a long illness. Much history is recorded in what was once just a small fishing village.

Bordeira

Bordeira (not to be confused with Bordeira near Sao Bras Aportal) is in Western Algarve. It is perhaps best known for its huge beach and sand dunes, popular with surfers who visit Praia da Bordeira for its winds and large waves. Few would venture a couple of kilometres inland to the little village itself. The main road by which you enter Bordeira is a fairly new one; it is wide and planted with rows of palms and flowerbeds. In front you cannot miss the small church: it is said to date from before the 1755 earthquake. The inside is stunning, with a heavily carved and gilded wooden centrepiece. The church is dedicated to the patron, our Lady of Incarnation. The small village sits in a basin surrounded by protected green countryside.

Unlike other small villages that are just whitewashed, Bordeira has many houses that are whitewashed but with vibrant colors picking out any features the building has.

Many small cobblestone roads, planted with orange and lemon trees, give the feeling of a traditional village. Some of the houses sit staggered high above one another. There is a café/bar aptly named Café da Bordeira, which offers light snacks and a limited lunch. There is a shop and other restaurants used by the locals. It is not surprising that there are not many ruins in the village, as it is a thriving little community; even what was once the communal bake oven/house has now been converted into living accommodation. The area is a green agricultural one, known for growing figs. Outside of the village, there is a surfing camp.

Burgau

Burgau is a small village in the Western Algarve; it is often seen as the Algarve's version of Cornwall in England. It is a picturesque village that still has a thriving fishing population: fishermen can still be seen repairing nets and lobster pots.

The village is very steep, many streets are cobbled, and some of the narrow pavements look like they might be private. But most will join the main roads in the village. There are many steps and steep climbs: if disabled or with limited mobility, you can still enjoy Burgau as there are many dedicated blue badge parking spaces down at the bottom near the beach. The beach is more like a cove bay being surrounded by large cliffs; one even resembles a pyramid in shape.

The beach is sheltered in a bay, with golden sand. Caution is needed with young children as the tide can come in fast and covers most of the beach. Caution is also need when parking down on the beach slops, as the tide has been known to cover vehicles.

Burgau has plenty of parking at the top of the village. Starting at the top gives opportunity to explore whilst making your way down to the many bars and good quality restaurants. Like most places, if you want to sit with front side views of the village and with sea views then expect to pay a little more for snacks and drinks. But the sea view is well worth it: it feels like you could be in the Mediterranean.

Those wanting a cheaper quality lunch or snack have a good choice at the top of the village. Atomik is one such place that has a modern theme and is clean. Just further along from Atomik is one of the largest hotels/restaurants, with a very colonial frontage. It was featured in the filming of 'One Foot in the Algarve' (part of the BBC television comedy drama series 'One Foot in the Grave', back in the 1990s).

Overall the village has much charm with many whitewashed cottages and townhouses; it offers plenty to do and has many quality gift shops, mini supermarkets.

Carrapateira

Carrapateira in the Western Algarve is a small village set within the Costa Vicentina Natural Park, which is a protected area of national beauty; Carrapateira comes under the main municipal of Aljezur. The village is a small one but has bars which cater for the surfing population that visit the village during surfing season. They have held national competitions which attract surfers from across the globe; some record-breaking waves have been recorded. Carrapateira village has a couple of restaurants well known for their fresh grilled fish. The few bars that are dotted around the centre are based on surfing themes. Carrapateira has a municipal daily market for fresh produce including fresh fish brought in from Lagos. Opposite across the main square sits the local school with its shaped parapet wall; this seems a common feature on older school houses across the Algarve.

There are the remains of a windmill that still has its wooden sail structure, but sadly it is privately owned so cannot be visited. Carrapateira has shops that sell surfing equipment as well as another shop that has basic everyday items. Overall it makes a good stop-off place to meet with other surfers, or just watch the world go by with a coffee or beer. You will find there are some artists that work in the village; it holds local events that gather locals from other surrounding villages. It would be best to ask a local bar or restaurant owner, as they would know when the events take place and it would unlikely be covered in any tourist office in the region. The village falls under the parish of Bordeira.

With Praia Bordeira being the nearest beach to the village of Carrapateira, it is the many sand dunes which give a clue that it is a windy beach. It has some great coastline with stunning walkways. Some say it is the best long beach of the Algarve, with its limestone backdrop cliffs. It is easy to see why it is so popular with surfers.

Carvoeiro

Carveoiro is in the Western Algarve but is almost in the Central Algarve, with the EN125 road running along the edge of the town. Lagoa district has some of the best water parks and golf courses for the area. There is a large old Adega (wine co-operative) just near the traffic lights in Lagoa, one of the first of its size for Portugal. Around 65 years of age, it is well worth a visit to sample and buy wines of the local regions.

Whilst on the way to Carvoeiro, there is a good choice of supermarkets – Pingo Doce, Intermache, and Aldi – where you can get fresh fish and meat. Carvoeiro has very picturesque views and is well known for its coastal cave trips by the local fishermen who know the waters very well. The main small beach is directly off the main road that circles the Town. With most beaches in the Algarve, Carvoeiro has a wheelchair/pushchair-friendly decking and access to its sandy beach.

Carvoeiro has many good restaurants and a number can be found on what is known as 'restaurant hill'. For most of the year the town is quiet. Peak season gets busy due to the fact it offers lots of holiday rental properties in the nearby hamlet of Sesmarinas, just off towards the east of Carvoeiro. It is the tourism from the 1960s that turned a sleeping fishing village into the town it has become today.

Carvoeiro is a picturesque fishing village that over the years has become one of the favourites with tourists. Carvoeiro today is an area of expensive villas and comfortable holiday apartments, with golf courses and nearby water parks. To the east is the small and attractive village of Porches that dates back to the Roman period. Unfortunately the earthquake of 1755 destroyed Carvoeiro's ancient castle and also the original parish church that is believed to have dated back to the 16th century.

Carvoeiro beaches are some of the most 'picture postcard' in the Algarve although not all are easily accessible.

Carvoeiro town consists of backstreets and steep roads. Fishing is still a thriving industry with many boats that land on the main beach to offload the catch of the day, normally before 10 am. When walking and exploring the backstreets, evidence of Roman habituation can be found, with remains of old walls from the period. There are remains of a fort on the outskirts of the town but it would go unnoticed unless you seek out the history of the town. One thing that is also lacking is any main church, which shows how small the original village was.

Well worth a visit out of town is the lighthouse, not so much for the lighthouse itself but for the amazing blow holes that surround it. These are huge holes, naturally formed, which have worn away the rock over the many years. They are fenced off for safety. When a strong tide comes in, sea water explodes high into the air, making a spectacular sight.

Estombar

Estombar in the Western Algarve lays to the south off the EN125. Estombar comes under the district of Lagoa, even though is closer to Portimao. This is because rivers act as boundaries. Estombar was given town status in 1991. The nearby river of Rio Arade has salt fields that are highly prized in the Algarve and can be seen from the road when crossing the bridge. The main church of Estombar, Igreja Matriz, sits proudly at the top of the town with its twin bell towers, although only one tower has bells: it was more important for the architectural look rather than both towers to have bells. The church can be seen from the road before entering the town.

On entering Estombar there is a large well-kept mature park with Children's play area, whilst across the road on the corner is the large indoor daily municipal market with fresh fish, bread and fruit and vegetables. Heading up towards the centre, it has many narrow streets as expected from any Algarvian town, with the odd merchant's house. The main church sits on a large square made of cobblestones.

There are panoramic views of the surrounding countryside and salt beds with views across to Portimao. Estombar offers some good restaurants with traditional decorated coloured fronts. In addition there are small bars/cafés. There are outside seating terraces just off the church square. Further up toward the urbanized part of the town sits a small bar. Outside daily is a mule and traditional hand decorated cart that stands in the shade, waiting to take its owner home.

There is a large events building on the eastern side of the town, used for fairs are events. If you are taking the turning on the right, the road runs alongside it. You will head out towards a very famous vineyard, Quinta Dos Vales, owned by the well known artist Karl Heinz, which is open to the public for wine tastings and function events. Life-size works from artists are on display, from giant hippos to elephants in a tree and hand decorated cows. The vineyard has produced many award-winning wines, but also has a petting zoo, with pot belly pigs, donkey, goats, deer, etc. Entrance to walk around is free.

The town has a railway station that sits just the other side of the main road when entering Estombar. Just further up the road towards Lagao is the popular slide and splash water park, and three nearby golf courses.

Ferragudo

Ferragudo is the 'Cornish' town of the Algarve, and a picture postcard one at that. If you are coming from Faro on the EN125, the turn off is just before the Portimao Bridge.

When you arrive, park at the top of the hill, with the town facing across the river, it just beckons you down to wander around such a beautiful town. Just as a short time ago as 1999 it was still a village, then the same year it was named as a town.

Ferragudo is becoming one of the most visited areas in the Algarve, with its Sunday flea market along the riverfront and the small cobbled square (Praça Rainha Dona Leonor) with its cafés and bars. What better way to sit and relax while watching the buzz from those hunting out a bargain? The town sits on the river Arade with view across to Portimao. Now resized, the port can take big cruise liners; you often see them moored across the river, almost as big as the building they sit next to. The town was once a thriving fishing village, and the activity still exists with the lobster pots and baskets stacked near the end of the riverfront. Restaurants offer spectacular views while eating lunch; in the evening there are the lights on the boats sparkling in the water's reflection, as well as views of the eastern side of the Fort of Sao Joao de Arade. Heading towards town, you will find the cobblestone backstreets with rows of small fishing houses; the odd merchant's house stands out, with decorated parapet walls and wrought ironwork over the doors and windows. You will see signs of billboards selling new builds; these are on the outskirts of the town, so will never take away the character and charm the town holds. With Praia da Angrinha beach nearest to the village you get the full front view of the Fort. It dates from the 15th century, with later additions in the 18th century. It was one of two forts built, the other being on the Portimao side, giving great defences to the river mouth. When the fort came to the end of its use it was sold into private hands. It remains so today and is not open to the public.

The town offers many restaurants used by locals, hidden on the back roads. Fish soup is one to look out for as the town seems to favour it; it can be eaten as a starter or main course. As the town heads uphill, with the church towards the top, you will come across gift shops and handcrafts on offer as well. Moving away from the town centre, you will see many villas overlooking the lighthouse down a one-way lane towards the coast on Ponta do Altar. For those who like walking it is possible to do so from the town, with the furthest beach being Praia dos Caneiros. This is easily found, as the council has painted arrows from the town along the coast for you to follow. When you get to Ferragudo lighthouse there is a panoramic view of Portimao harbour across the river, with Monchique Mountain in the background: one of the best opportunities for photographing sea and land views. Ferragudo has two good beaches, both very large so that there is no overcrowding in peak season: Praia Grande and Praia do Pintadinho. Ferragudo has much to offer, with good shopping and a nearby large Lidl.

Lagoa

Lagoa in the Western Algarve is one of those towns (it does in fact have city status) that can easily be missed due to the fact that the EN125 runs through it. On approaching the town from the east, you first come across traffic lights on a decorative traffic island, with statues and water features. Left, you will see the Parque Municipal, a large exhibitions park where many events are held each year, including the largest for the Algarve: the Fatacil fair, held every August over a ten-day period.

Taking the right-hand road leads to the town's centre; the other road leads to Silves. Lagoa is a lot larger than it looks, with many small alleyways and narrow cobblestone roads. There are many little garden areas with seating, including a shrine to Our Lady (Lady of the Light). Another garden is the War Memorial Park with a dedicated large pink granite war memorial. You will also find opposite the main church (Igreja Matriz) a small records Museum: Arqivo (Portuguese for 'file'). This has impressive glass frontage with a large handmade tile decoration from the nearby Porches pottery. There is a large pedestrian area decorated with black and white cobblestones with rows of shops and cafés offering outside seating areas, leading towards another park garden with a bandstand.

Lagoa offers some of the best water parks as well as golf courses. The large old Adega (wine co-operative) just near the traffic lights towards Carveoiro is well worth a visit to sample and buy wines of the regions. With the main town opposite and its population of around 20,000, Lagoa may be small but still offers heritage buildings which have been renovated for cultural uses: the municipal library and the Convento de São José (St Joseph Convent). The decorated cobbled main strip in Lagoa has some nice restaurants and plenty of bars-cafés to while away an hour over a coffee. You will also discover some of the gift shops selling hand-painted tiles, a tradition fast disappearing. Lagoa still offers a host of events each year, having the Fatacil show ground (Parque de Feiras e Exposições de Lagoa) and holding numerous fairs and shows covering local art and crafts and including live music with traditional songs.

The large August Fatacil fair offers petting animals, motor shows, boats and arts and crafts, even down to making a stained glass window. Or you could observe a cobbler making shoes. The park also holds a monthly flea market and undercover antiques fair. Just further down near the commercial park is the main monthly market, which is held for foods, linen and clothes. (See markets.)

Just past the main traffic lights on the turn off for Carveoiro you will find a large building displaying the words 'Adega Cooperative'. This is one of the first adega buildings of its size in Portugal, built over 65 years ago. It is still a functioning working winery and is now known as Unica. In the past you might not have noticed the building as a working adega, but since July 2013 a new coat of paint brings the adega to your attention. Worth visiting, it offers good regional wines in the smaller shop situated to the right of the main building. The adega has been put up for sale but is still open to the public.

Lagoa Museum

Lagos

Lagos in the Western Algarve was the main city for the while Algarve back in the 16th century.

You can't help but get into that holiday mode, with its marina along the front. It is just what you would expect: sun, sea and a picturesque place that looks affluent with its million-pound yachts and boats. One can dream of gracing the high seas on crystal clear waters, with a glass of something in one hand, or even a fishing rod in the other.

Well, easily possible, as you can easily find many boat trips for the day to take in the Algarve's coastline whilst sunbathing on deck. If fishing takes your fancy you can go for the day or half day with a BBQ on board and eating your catch for lunch. The main town offers a vibrant array of shops, cafés, bars and restaurants. It was once said that in 1587 Francis Drake failed to raid Lagos; if only they had the bakeries then that they have now, he would have had something to fight for, as the pastel de natas (custard tarts in flaky pastry) are not to be missed, taken with a coffee in one of the many bars before you set off exploring Lagos.

Even if you are not a history buff you can't help but observe the culture Lagos had back in the 15th century, with its buildings dating back to 1445, including Europe's first ever building used solely for the purpose of selling slaves, hence slave markets. It's worth wandering through the backstreets as you never know what you will come across, from the golden Church of Santo Antonio to hunting out the little bakers that sell all sorts of pies – steak and kidney, cheese and onion – and quiches.

Little changes over time when it comes to marinas, but now it's more up-to-date: instead of 800 galleons from the Armada led by Dom Sebastiao in 1578, it now houses around the same number of luxury boats and yachts. The traditional decorated fishing boat has always stood the test of time and will do so for years to come, offering trips to nearby caves. Lagos has seen its moments in history, including even a visit from Columbus. With all this history behind it and its important buildings which have stood the test of time, Lagos is what you want to make it, from strolling along the marina before heading to a restaurant to watch the sunset, down to bars and clubs which stay open all night, giving you time to leave to see the sunrise. Those who enjoy photo opportunities should visit the Fort (Forte da Bandeira), built in the 17th Century.

Check the tourist office to see what events are going on then head to the cultural centre in the square, as many exhibitions are laid on throughout the year.

Mexilhoeira Grande

Mexilhoeira Grande in the Western Algarve comes under the parish of the nearby city of Portimao. The village is known for its archeological finds, located on a hill with views over the river and Portimao from the top of the village which now sits between the EN125 and the A22. A short distance from Mexilhoeira is the Ribeira de Odiaxere, well known for its salt fields, where the salt is diverted from the river into special prepared salt beds. These are still harvested by hand using wooden rakes to pile salt crystals into rows which are then left to dry by the sun.

It is probably the second biggest salt producer in the Algarve next to Faro, as its salt is highly prized; Mexilhoeira was in the past well known for the collection of oysters, clams, and mussels harvested from the nearby mud flats on the marshland below the village.

When you enter the village, with a gentle climb to the top, bronze statues to celebrate well-known locals can be found whilst on the way.

Mexilhoeira Grande has great community spirit, with many tiled benches placed outside one of the smaller chapels. There is also a seating area at the large church at the top of the village, normally occupied by locals chatting in the late afternoons; this offers fantastic river and coastal views across to Portimao. The church bell can be heard for miles around, whilst the carved stone church doorway dates from the 18th century.

The village offers many good restaurants that offer an excellent dish of the day for around €7 with all included. There are numerous bars dotted around the village as well as a mini supermarket. It is well worth visiting as the many buildings all offer something different in the way of architecture. The village is a little cooler in the summer months with a welcoming breeze coming from the coast. However, some days the smell from the mud flats can be unbearable when the tide is out. It is probably better to park at the first opportunity, as many of the roads can be narrow and one-way streets.

Monchique

Monchique is the Algarve's only official mountain, being 902 metres above sea level; a visit makes an ideal day-trip, taking a break from beaches. Monchique is set in the Serra de Monchique borders, towards the Alentejo region where the Algarve ends and Central Portugal begins, with its thick forest all the way to the border.

Check the skies when planning your visit; you don't want a wasted journey as Monchique can often be cloudy with poor visibility.

It is a good easy drive on the main road to Monchique: the drive up gives the feel of an adventure ahead. The road is lined with eucalyptus trees and yellow flowering mimosa trees. On the road up is the small hamlet called Caldas de Monchique. This is the natural spring spa reputed to have healing properties, first witnessed in the Roman period. There are two further hot spring sites, one named Fonte Santa south of Picota and hidden in a valley.

Caldos de Monchique has a small chapel and many unusually designed houses; with restaurants and bars to stop off for lunch, as those at the top of Monchique in the main square are mostly snack bars. Caldos' small hamlet offers a building that is open nearly all year round with different events, mainly art and craft exhibitions. The area has many picnic areas to enjoy so it is well worth thinking of taking a picnic and having lunch in its beautiful surroundings.

As you head towards Monchique you will find on the right-hand side Parque da Mina. Open all year, this has a waterfall at the entrance. Well worth visiting, this takes you back in time with its many displayed themes and vintage items.

Following the road's many sharp bends something appears round every corner: look out for the man and his donkey. He will let you sit on its back for a photo opportunity. Further along are large pottery shops with hand-painted tiles and other gifts. These are well worth a browse as they are slowly declining in numbers across the Algarve. On reaching the top, you will find that the square has undergone a revamp so even if you have been in the last few years it is well worth a return. The first thing you will notice is the top of a huge tree, a member of the pine family, sitting in the ground of a small park. In the centre square they have restored a Nora (well) which has tin buckets that go round to fill up water buckets, now turned into a fun water feature. In the past it was driven by donkeys which would pull up water for up to 10 hours a day

Strolling around you'll find lifelike bronze figures of adults and children. On your walkabout, you will also find the working public laundry: no washing machines here. It is still used by the locals to wash and scrub their clothes and linen before taking it back home to dry. From the town looking up into the hillside you will spot the ruin of a 17th-century Franciscan monastery. You can have a wander around. A nearby house in the grounds, lived in by a family, offers a few vegetables grown in the gardens for sale to keep the geese and other birds that live around the ruins.

Monchique has many cobbled backstreets with little galleries and handmade gifts. Many of its streets are unlike anything that you will find elsewhere in the Algarve; some can be very steep but they are well worth it for the dramatic views.

On sale is a clear spirit called "Medronho"; known locally as fire water, it is a type of schnapps. Distilled from the red fruit of the arbtutus tree/bush – rather like a lychee in appearance – it is very much an acquired taste with quite a kick to it. As the area is also surrounded with cork trees and woodlands, cork products can be found in the gift shops. Cork is so hard-wearing that they make hats, wallets and bags from it; the cork industry is still a thriving one today. Monchique, being little changed for years, still thrives in its own community, with pig farming, bee keeping, vegetable growing on the fertile soil on the lower hills. It is also known for its drinkable spring water.

The square has a handful of restaurants; you will also find an excellent restaurant on the way down Fosa da Banha, serving homemade bread and offering beautiful views when eating on the open outside terrace.

In 2013 Monchique saw the British Prime Minister take a holiday with his family, so no doubt it will see many more visitors in the future.

Odeceixe

Odeceixe is one of the last towns in the Western Algarve, coming under the district of Aljezur. The Ribera de Seixe river separates Odeceixe and the town of Sines – the start of the silver coast with its parkland protected areas – and the start of Alentejo. Seen by some as a bit out of the way when it comes to tourism, it is a real hidden gem well worth travelling to. Not that far from Ajezur and Sines, Odeceixe is reached by the EN120 when exiting Aljezur. The main road to the town is on a sharp bend, with a view of the town and its windmill that sits on the tallest hill overlooking Odeceixe and is still in working order. You can drive up to the top where you will also pass one of the town churches. The windmill symbol is shown on Odeceixe's coat of arms.

The town has much to offer: you will find a daily indoor market offering fresh fish and daily produce. A few doors away from the post office is a popular café/bar in the middle called Snack Bar Mercado, used by locals as the area offers free WI-FI for those who feel the need of the internet. There are parking places in front of the market or a large car park on the outskirts of the town.

Many of the streets are cobbled, which adds to the character and charm of the place. In the centre, in a small square with a stone water fountain, there are plenty of public benches offering seating surrounded with planters filled with flowers. Odeceixe surprisingly has around 12-16 different restaurants and bars. Some offer seating inside or on small terraces that form part of the cobbled roads. You should take care with small children as the town looks as if it is for pedestrians only, but in fact it is well used by traffic. The buildings are a mixture, including the odd merchant's house with tiled fronts with cast iron and stone Juliet balconies. There are plenty of shops for all your grocery needs as well gift shops. These offer more handmade items, rather than the usual seaside town gifts that you find everywhere. The town has a good nightlife with bars holding music evenings on different nights of the week, from fado to small bands. Odeceixe offers an ideal holiday location with hotels in the centre and smaller B&Bs in surrounding areas. The nearby beach is popular with naturists as it is one of the few official naturist beaches in the Algarve.

Odiaxere

Odiaxere in the Western Algarve is a small village under the parish of Lagos: it has its charms like other Algarve villages, but the fact that the EN125 runs right through the middle means that Odiaxere appears to be left off the tourist map. You will be very hard pushed to find any information on Odiaxere.

The village offers a good stop-off point, for many reasons. Odiaxere has plenty of good restaurants, with the food being more traditional than the nearby coastal town of Lagos. A lunch can be as little as €6 including wine in the local restaurants, with fresh fish arriving daily (except Sundays). Odiaxere has a good size indoor daily fish and produce market, with the bonus of not having to join long queues in the summer months. The outside of the market is decorated with a hand-painted tiled panel on the walls. There are stone tables and benches that are enjoyed by locals who play dominoes and cards in the shade; they can be used for a picnic lunch.

Odiaxere has a garden square off the main road, with plenty of seating around a water feature; there are public toilets that are clean and open daily.

One house stands out from the square, an impressive tiled frontage with a cast iron balcony. This may well have been a merchant's house as was normal to show off the wealth of the owner. From the square sits the Igreja Matriz Odiaxere church with its impressive bell tower and cockerel weathervane. The church was rebuilt after the 1755 earthquake; the impressive stone-carved doorway survived. Dating from the late 17th to

18th century, this is a favourite with artists and photographers. The village has a river named after it: Ribeiro de Odiaxere, which runs to the ocean. Odiaxere plays a large role in the salt industry; the many salt beds are skimmed regularly for the salt, which is then left to dry in the sun, forming white salt crystals. These are then gathered into cloth sacks. The village has a large inland lake with many walking areas and wildlife.

Portimao Bridge

Portimao

Portimao, being on the south coast of Portugal comes under the Western Algarve. It is the second largest city after Faro, with a population of around 55,000 inhabitants.

From the EN125, you drive across the impressive bridge which crosses the Arade River and was finished in 1991. On the left-hand side you will see what appear to be people: they are scarecrows to protect the salt fields. Salt is gathered into piles in the warmer months, and then loaded into sacks by hand to be taken away for cleaning. The bridge gives views towards Portimao harbour, which has the capacity for large cruise ships.

Like many towns in Portugal, the earthquake of 1755 destroyed much of the city and little was done to rebuild for almost 100 years. The waterways soon began to regain imports and exports. In 1924 Portimao became a city and has not looked back since, becoming one of the Algarve's most loved cities for tourists.

The new marina has put Portimao back on the map: it is now the epicentre of water sports in the Algarve as well as fishing day-trips. You can even go dolphin watching. Portimao has in recent years been focusing on sinking redundant ships and vessels to encourage scuba diving, making it one of the top spots for this in the Algarve. Sinking the vessels is not just about scuba diving but creating a coral reef to bring back natural wildlife. There are river boat tours to the historic town of Silves, with the stunning castle that dominates the town.

The city's streets are full, with plenty to see; in the centre is Largo 1 Dezembro, a paved garden square, well shaded for those hot summer days. The large building nearby is the birthplace of Manuel Teixeira Gome, the 7th president of Portugal and a renowned writer. The square is surrounded by plenty of bars and cafés making it a good resting place for coffee, and with the large nearby fountain giving a cooling effect.

Portimao Marina

You cannot help noticing the seating benches with hand-painted tiles covering the history of Portugal's main events. The city has good pedestrian areas closed to the traffic, and only open at rush hour. You will find Portimao is a traditional city and its many bars, restaurants and pasterias offer an amazing choice of cakes and pastries. Portimao is popular with the Chinese, with many shops and restaurants for those wanting something different.

Portimao Town Hall

Whilst touring the backstreets it's worth looking up to see the ornate ironwork balconies and stoneware urns that sit on the parapet walls and hand-painted tiled façades. On the edge of the town is the large municipal indoor market, open every day for fresh fish and daily produce.

If wanting to try local cuisine without eating in a restaurant you will find many sell take-away. Popular with office workers, these range from pasta dishes to suckling roasted pig, normally sold by weight.

A visit to Portimao is not complete without a stroll along the 1½-kilometre marina front, with an assortment of yachts and boats.

Trains: Portimao has a train station, which connects the town with most other towns and resorts along the Algarve coast. Faro airport is approximately 1 hour 20 minutes away by train, while Lagos is a mere 20 minutes away.

Sailing: Portimao is the host and venue of many prestigious sailing events including the annual Portimao Portugal Match Cup event, part of the Match racing tour.

Power boating: Portimao's coastline has also been the host for the sport of power boating: the Portuguese Grand Prix of the Sea, run by Powerboat P1 as part of its international championships.

Motorsport: Inland near Portimao is the Autodromo International do Algarve, a race and test circuit officially recognized for the highest categories both for cars and motorcycles.

Portimao main church

Portimao Square Fountain

Praia da Luz

Praia da Luz, in the Western Algarve, is a small coastal village that comes under the district of Lagos. It was very much a fishing village until discovered by tourism is the 1960s. When approaching Luz from the west, coming out of Burgau, you notice the first signs of the village with a breathtaking view of the backdrop of the rocks that form the well-protected bay of Praia da Luz. In front of the view are the many modern villas and apartments that have grown over the years. One good thing is that there are no high-rise apartment blocks to spoil the village. You can still see the many older houses that keep to the tradition of whitewashing cottages for which the Algarve is known. It is well worth parking as soon as you can, as the village is quiet compact and the deeper in you go, the harder to find parking spaces.

Praia da Luz has many shops and bars and restaurants to cope with the large number of people that head to the beaches in the summer months. There is easy walking around the town, with only four main roads, and the beach is just 200 metres from the central street. The village has a small but impressive church with intricate carved gilt wooden altar. At the rear of the church is what looks like easy parking, but caution! Many of these parking spaces are strictly for residents of nearby properties and you could find your car being towed away. Past the church towards the waterfront is a small square with seating offering shade as well as a great view of both sides of the village, one half being rock, the other being the beach. The promenade has good access for pushchairs and wheelchairs. The pavement is decorated with traditional flat cobblestones with black and white patterns. There is a good choice of small restaurants along the promenade; prices are good for a lunch. Just along the front, you will find the remains of a Roman bathhouse which dates from around the 4th century, accessed by a doorway entrance and open daily from 10am to 5pm during peak season. The beach is a sheltered one being in a bay; when the tide goes out shallow rock pools are left, ideal for children to paddle or sit in. Further along the beach turns to rock, popular with snorkelers. Water sports can be seen further along the eastern side of the beach.

Praia da Luz church

Praia da Rocha

Praia da Rocha in the Western Algarve comes under the district of Portimao. The town has much to offer, from five-star hotels and a casino to smaller holiday apartments. Praia da Rocha underwent an extensive upgrading in the last few years and offers great walking areas with black and white traditional cobbled walkways.

Many of the main roads have dedicated cycle paths. When entering from the west, you will discover a roundabout with a large impressive water feature, its water jets reaching eight metres high. The main features of Praia da Rocha have to be the fantastic coastal views and huge wide beach. Walking decking runs the full length of the beach down towards the rock caves, making access easy for pushchairs and wheelchairs. Even in the busy months of July and August you will always find plenty of space on the beach. Praia da Rocha has much history, with the 16th century fortress Santa Catarina de Ribamar at the eastern end overlooking the marina with views across to Ferragudo. On the Ferragudo side is the fortress Soa Joao Arade: the two forts protected the river mouth, making it almost impossible to invade during the 16th and 17th centuries.

The Small Praia da Rocha marina has many townhouses, all painted the same colour, giving a good backdrop to the views across the river. There are great opportunities for the many boat rides on offer. One of the ships that offers such trips is the traditional wooden pirate galleon ship that is often seen sailing out of the harbour into the ocean. The main promenade road, which is one-way, offers payment parking in bays along the road. Free parking can be found towards the western side near the water fountain roundabout. There are a few dedicated disabled parking places as well as public toilets near the tourist police station that offer wheelchair access. Praia da Rocha has around 30 restaurants and bars that cater for all styles of food as well as catering for families on a budget. All the top hotels offer dining for non-patrons, not forgetting those many restaurants down on the beach reached easily by the decking. You may even come across a certain restaurant and bar which opened in the 1970s. The owners have a blue and yellow macaw parrot that likes to walk around freely and enjoys the odd tipple of beer. The town has plenty of smaller supermarkets for those self-catering. Portimao is just up the road, with its new shopping centre that opened in 2013: it is easy to visit by bus or taxi, costing just a few euros. Praia da Rocha has a good safety record for tourist crime. However, this is not the case for traffic and pedestrian accidents: this is because the decorated cobbled pavements blend in with the cobbled roads. Care is needed with younger children as there can be difficulty telling the road from the pavement along the one-way promenade road running along the front.

Sagres

Sagres in the Western Algarve comes under the district of Vila do Bispo. Mentino Sagres and most would think of the beer with the same name. The beer was named after the town as a symbol of stability and long standing, like the landmark of the fort (Fortaleza de Sagres) and the rock cliffs it stands on. It is the most southwesterly point of Europe: Henry the Navigator ordered the siting and building of the fortress in the 15th century to protect the strategic coastal position, with the coves that offer shelter for shipping during strong storms.

Sagres is popular with those wanting to reach this furthest point and visit both the fort and lighthouse of Ponta de Sagres (Farol da Ponta de Sagres) in nearby Cape St Vincent. The lighthouse is perhaps not as old as tourists imagine, having only been built in 1958 on the same spot as the previous one from the 1890s. Today the light can be seen from over 20 kilometres away. Due to it being the most south-westerly point in Europe, during the Roman period it was thought to be the end of the world, with the sun sinking into the sea at the end of every day. Sagres is small but worth walking around, with the calm clear harbour down below with its two piers. The large building Docapesca at the beginning of the harbour wall houses the fish auctions and fish processing, with up to five tons of fish sorted for distribution a day.

Bronze statue of Henry the Navigator

In the town stands a large bronze statue of Henry the Navigator, who was the originator of early explorations from Europe to much of the rest of the world, which enabled important trade with other continents. Sagres has a small sheltered cobbled square set with palms; there are plenty of cafés and snack bars offering lunches. Further along are other restaurants with views overlooking the rugged rocks with sea views. Despite being a rocky coastal village Sagres has a golden sandy beach with its sheltered bay providing calmer waters than those sought by surfers just further along; it does make an ideal beach to spend the day. The beach is located just off the roundabout before the fort on the Rua da Fortaleza road. For those wanting to visit the fort, just continue a little further: the fort will be seen straight ahead. On entering through a tunnel passageway you will see a large pebble circle nearly 43 metres in diameter. Little is known about its age, use or origin; it was only discovered in the 1920s. There have been debates questioning whether it could be a rose compass (Rosa dos Ventos), but this has 40 sections rather than the normal 32. The fort not only gives great photo opportunities but you can also say that you have visited the most southwesterly point in Europe. Those who love nature will find much to enjoy, as Sagres sits in the national park with many walks where little-seen flora and fauna can be encountered.

Sagres Cliffs

Sagres Fort

Vila do Bispo

Vila do Bispo in the Western Algarve is a small village that comes under the district of Lagos. Its claim to fame was that in 1543, a local from the village, Fernão Mendes Pinto, was one of the first Europeans to land in Japan. In 1992 a new square was built nearer the outskirts of the village, to celebrate the twinning of the town he visited, Tanegashima. The square is officially named praca de Tanegashima (Tashegashima Square).

This new square has transformed Vila do Bispo's popularity: back in the 1930s its population was over 6,000 but its numbers declined for almost 80 years. Vila do Bispo still has the little garden square, once the centre of the village, which is situated near the main church (Nossa Senhora da Conceiçao). This, dating from the 16th century, is one of the few buildings which remains from before the 1755 earthquake.

The village has great charm with many narrow streets with cottages and merchants' houses. It has an extra feeling of time standing still, due to the older-style streetlamps used in the centre. Towards the church are cobblestone roads that are a very steep climb and are just wide enough for one car's width. The buildings differ greatly, from the restored remains of a windmill when first entering the town to the modern buildings set around the new square; the village's expanse has even incorporated a huge sculpture with a garden on the main roundabout.

There are many restaurants, with a good varied choice from restaurant to restaurant. A popular one that fits in with the new square is the Ribeira do Poco, with its marble and stone sculptures sitting on its parapet wall.

There is plenty of parking in the village and it is popular with motorhomes due to the easy parking near the new square. Vila do Bispo has many cafés and bars scattered around; it is a good stop-off point as it offers easy access. Just off the EN125, on the outskirts of the village, are a petrol station and a large supermarket. There is a monthly market held every first Thursday of the month.

Vila do Bispo is of historic importance, as surrounding the area are stones that date back to the Stone Age period. These are called menhirs in Portuguese. They are not only important to the Algarve but are protected; you will see signs that indicate where they are as well as tourist information on them.

Algarve Cities, Towns and Villages: Distance Ch

																											Albufeira
																										Alcoutim	131
																									Aljezur	201	80
																								Alvor	47	158	37
																							Armacao de Pera	25	68	139	18
																						Carvoeiro	18	17	60	151	30
																					Castro Marim	111	99	123	161	40	91
																				Faro	51	60	48	67	110	91	40
																			Lagoa	55	96	5	13	12	55	146	25
																		Lagos	25	60	136	30	38	17	30	171	50
																	Loule	69	44	16	58	49	37	56	99	98	29
																Monchique	73	38	29	84	140	34	42	25	68	175	54
															Monte Gordo	134	56	130	105	50	9	110	94	117	160	49	90
														Olhao	42	92	24	88	63	88	43	68	56	75	118	83	48
													Portimao	71	113	21	52	17	8	63	119	13	21	4	47	154	33
												Praia de Luz	26	97	139	47	78	9	34	89	145	39	47	26	39	180	59
											Praia da Rocha	29	3	74	116	24	55	20	11	66	122	16	24	5	50	157	36
										Quarteira	56	79	53	30	72	74	11	70	45	22	73	50	39	57	100	113	17
									Quinta do Lago	10	61	84	58	35	77	79	16	75	50	27	78	55	43	62	105	114	35
								Sagres	108	103	53	28	50	121	163	71	102	33	58	113	169	63	71	50	43	204	83
							S.B.Messines	83	43	37	36	59	33	55	97	43	35	50	25	47	98	30	20	37	80	138	25
						S.B.Alportel	48	115	29	24	68	91	65	17	43	86	13	87	51	17	43	62	49	69	112	83	42
					Silves	65	17	66	58	52	19	42	16	71	113	26	52	33	8	63	104	13	18	20	63	154	33
				Tavira	92	22	86	142	56	51	95	118	92	21	21	113	35	109	84	29	23	89	77	96	139	63	63
			Vale de Lobo	52	54	25	39	104	4	6	57	80	54	31	73	75	12	71	46	23	74	51	39	58	101	104	31
		Vila do Bispo	94	132	56	105	73	10	98	93	43	18	40	111	153	61	92	23	48	103	159	53	61	40	33	194	73
	V.R.St.Antonio	155	75	23	115	45	97	165	179	74	118	141	115	44	5	136	58	132	107	52	4	112	96	119	162	44	92
Vilamoura	81	82	10	58	42	27	26	92	12	4	45	68	42	39	79	63	14	59	34	29	80	39	27	46	89	120	13

Food and Drink

Meat names translated

Frango: Chicken
Perú: Turkey
Pato: Duck
Porco: Pork
Fiambre: Ham
Febras: Pork steak
Lombo de porco: Pork loin
Vaca: Beef
Bife de vaca (bem passado): Beef steak (well done)
Bife de vazia: Sirloin steak
Bifanas: Thin pork steaks
Bitoque: Minute steak
Picar: Mince
Vitela: Veal
Borrego: Lamb
Costeletas de Borrego: Lamb chops
Coelho: Rabbit.

Famous grilled chicken piri piri

Fish translation

Atum: Tuna
Bacalhau:Cod
Besugo: Sea bream
Carapau: Horse mackerel
Cavala: Mackerel
Cherne: Grouper
Choco: Cuttlefish
Dourada: Bream
Espadarte: Swordfish
Linguado: Sole
Lula: Squid
Moreia: Moray eel
Pargo: Red Snapper
Pescada: Hake
Polvo: Octopus
Robalo: Sea bass
Safio: Eel / Small conger
Salmão: Salmon
Salmonete: Mullet
Sardinha: Sardine
Sargo Porgy: Dourada
Tamboril: Monkfish

Shellfish translation

Ameijoa: Clam
Berbigão: Cockle
Búzio: Whelk
Camarão: Prawn
Carangueijo: Crab
Conquilha: Clam (small)
Lagosta: Lobster
Lingueirão: Clam razor
Mexhilhão: Mussel
Ostra: Oyster
Santola: Spider crab

Milk types

Semi desnatado: Semi skimmed
Meio da gordura: Half fat
Fresco: Fresh
Pasteurizado: Pasteurised
Gordo: Full fat

Herbs/Spices

Erva-doce: Anise
Manjericáo: Basil
Louro: Bay leaves
Alcaravia: Caraway
Pimenta-de-Caiena: Cayenne
Aipo: Celery seed
Piri piri: Chilli
Cebolinha: Chives
Canela: Cinnamon
Coentro: Coriander
Alho: Garlic
Sals: Parsley

Cooking terms

Grelhar: Grilling
Assar: Roasting
Cozer: Boiling
Estufar: Stewing

Cheese types

Velho: Old, vintage cheese of a few months
Curado, semi-curado: Cured, semi-cured
Amanteigado: Smooth spreading cheese
Mole/ de pasta mole, semi-mole: Soft, semi-soft
Duro/ de pasta dura, semi-duro: Hard, semi-hard
Leite de vaca: Cow's milk
Leite de ovelha ('o-vayl-yaâ'): Sheep's milk
Leite de cabra/cabreiro: Goat's milk
Cru: Raw
Picante: Spicy
Casca: Casing, wrapping, shell
Ligeiro/a: Light (in consistency)

Wines

This section is here to help you understand a little about the many great wines of Portugal. Whilst you may think you have never consumed a Portuguese wine before, many of you will have had a well-known wine that has been going for more than 50 years. That is of course the famous Mateus Rosé in its very distinctively shaped bottle.

Mateus is what most people conjure up when they think of the well-known Italian wine that came in a straw-covered bottle and sat on a restaurant table with a candle in, back in the 1970s. In a way you would be right to think so, as Mateus was a wine developed solely for the export market. Portugal led the way in inventing a new style of wine for export and became successful at the process. This short wine guide is not going to bore you nor turn you into a master of wines; it will help you choose the type of wine you would drink at home and dispel the myth about good cooperative wines being cheap and nasty because they are sold in a carton. First, let's start with a good, light, refreshing wine for which Portugal is well known. Most likely the largest quantity produced is Vinho Verde or 'green wine'. Although the name refers to green, nearly 80% of Vinho Verdes are reds; Vinho Verdes come from unripe (green) grapes, as the name implies.

Many Vinho Verdes traditionally come from the Douro region, but nowadays they seem to come from all over Portugal. For those of you who are not wine lovers, this is a good wine to introduce you to, with the start of something that will change your opinion on wine drinking. Vinho Verdes are light and refreshing, some with a light sparkle to them, as they are from the unripe grape having less sugar in the grape.

Most are less than 10% vol in alcohol. When driving on your travels, you will often see grape vines growing up high on pergolas; these are likely to be grapes for a Vinho Verde. Portugal wines had quality control 25 years before France even introduced the famous 'appellation controlée'. With this in mind you won't find any of the well-known vineyards putting less than 100% quality control into their wine.

If you come to Portugal during the harvest season, you will find towns and villages celebrating a joint venture. In all large supermarkets there will be displays of all the wines of the regions, along with the many regional cheeses, cured meats, and hams.

Algarve Wines

As the Algarve is perhaps the main holiday destination of Portugal, most people will just think of it as the holiday resort with sun, sea, and beaches. But it offers so much more, with over nine well-known wineries. But did you know many are open to the public, offering you an experience and great day out that you'll be glad you included in your holiday? Even if you have children don't be put off, as some, like Quinta dos Vales in Estombar near Portimao, have a mini zoo, great gardens and world of sculptures, from elephants to kissing hippos, and even dancing cows.

These open days can give even the novice a real eye-opener. Others, like Adega do Cantor in Guia in the Central Algarve, will give guided tours and explain every stage, from the picking of the grape from the vines to the production process. Then down to the best part of the tour: the tasting of its well-known medal-winning wines, from reds to rosés. Vida Nova wines are the joint effort of Sir Cliff Richard and Nigel Birch. Unlike many branded sauces and food products this is not a gimmick wine, as you will not see Cliff Richard's face plastered across the front label. Vida Nova is just coming to the 10-year mark and already has awards and medals for its outstanding contribution to the Portuguese wine market. Portugal today is well-established as one of the top ten wine-producing countries in the world.

Other Wineries in Algarve

Adega do Cantor (Guia)
Quinta do Frances (Silves)
Quinta do Morgado (Alvor)
Quinta da Vinha (Lagoa)
Monte da Casteleja (Lagos)
Quinta de Mata Mouros (Silves)
Quinta do Outeiro (Silves)
Quinta dos Vales (Estombar)

Below are some useful terms found on the labels of wine, also a few wine terms found on the bottle/carton.

Adega: Winery
Branco: White
Casta: Grape variety
Colheita: Vintage year
Espumante: Sparkling
Garrafeira: A reserva, either a red wine aged two years in a barrel / one year in a bottle, or a white wine aged six months in a barrel / six months in a bottle
Maduro: Mature
Quinta: Vineyard
Reserva: Good quality wine of a single vintage
Seco: Dry
Tinto: Red
Verde: Green or red wines that fall into the Vinho Verde category
Vinho: Wine

Douro Wines: These are fruity wines of excellent quality, and come from the same regions as port, with their strong colours. The white wines are also served with fish and pastes. The reds are served with game, fowl and strong cheeses.

Dão Wines: These have a low alcoholic content ranging from 10 to 13% volume. Having a fine and velvety flavour, the reds are often a good dark ruby colour, and best served with game, spicy meat and cheese. The whites are often crisp and light, with a citrus tone and very aromatic to the nose. Serve with game, grilled meats, strong cheeses of the region.

Alentejo Wines: The vineyards of the Alentejo are most famous for Borbas & Reguengos de Monsaraz, Vidigueira, Cuba and Alvito. The white wine production is larger than that of the reds but both types are ideal companions for the delicious regional cured meats and cheeses, ideal for light suppers.

Colares Wines: A good wine that is suitable and complements game and red meat. White is best served chilled with fish, pasta and a good selection of cheeses.

Bucelas Wines: Very acid when young, and can be dry once aged; ideal for BBQs and fish dishes.

Moscatel: A good old-fashioned dessert wine for dinner with guests. The wine produced from this grape is smooth and perfumed, like honey when it is five years old, but is richer and even more subtle after reaching a maturity of 20 years plus. Ideal with crepes filled with fresh fruits.

Algarve Wines: The new wines of Portugal: many make great light everyday drinking, with most being low in alcohol (volume of around 13%). Some great rosés are served before a meal or with starters; whites tend to be very refreshing, whilst the many reds hold their own up against the many great Portuguese wines. But they tend to be less heady, so are ideal for holiday consumption.

What to see and what's on

There are many markets for you to visit all over Portugal. Most villages will have a daily fixed market within a market building. But each will host a monthly market; this is where people come from afar to sell the many products of their region. Some can be as small as 15 stalls on the cobbled backstreets; the largest can be well over a 100 stalls. Larger markets will even cater for breakfast meals and early lunches, cooked over traditional charcoal stoves. They range from clothes shoes, leather goods to linens, fresh fruit and veg, regional cheeses, hams and cured meats to the traditional dried cod known as bacalhau; some will even have plants and livestock.

Markets in Algarve

Algoz	2nd Monday
Albufeira	1st & 3rd Tuesday
Alcantarilha	1st Friday
Aljezur	3rd Monday
Almancil	1st & 4th Sunday
Alvor	2nd Tuesday
Alte	3rd Thursday
Amexixal	1st Thursday
Azilheira	1st Thursday
Azinhal	Last Saturday
Benfim	1st Saturday
Boliqueime	Last Thursday
B.S.Joao	4th Sunday
B.S.Miguel	1st Monday
Budens	1st Tuesday
Castro Mirim	2nd Saturday
Cortelha	2nd Saturday
Estoi	2nd Sunday
Fuzeta	1st Thursday
Guia	3rd Friday
Lagoa	2nd Sunday
Lagos	1st Saturday
Loulé	Every Sunday
Messines	4th Monday
Moncarapacho	1st Sunday
Monchique	2nd Friday

Odiaxere	4th Monday
Paderne	1st Saturday
Pereiro	1st Saturday
Portimao	1st Monday
Quarteira	Every Wednesday
Quelfes	4th & 5th Sunday
Raposeira	1st Wednesday
Rogil	4th Sunday
Sagres	1st Friday
Sao Bras	Every Saturday
S.Catarina	4th Sunday
Silves	3rd Monday
S.Marcos	2nd Sunday
Tavira	3rd Saturday
Tunes	4th Saturday
Vaqueiros	2nd Thursday
Vila do Bispo	1st Thursday
V.N de Cacela	3rd Sunday

Algoz Monthly Market

Flea markets

Albufeira	3rd Saturday
Algoz	1st Saturday
Alcantarilha	2nd Saturday
Almancil	2nd & 5th Sunday
B.S.Joao	4th Sunday
Chinicato	2nd Sunday

Estombar	Last Sunday
Espiche	3rd Sunday
Ferragudo	2nd Sunday
Fuzeta	1st Sunday
Lagoa	4th Sunday
Monchique	4th Sunday
Monte Gordo	4th Saturday
Portimao	1st & 3rd Sunday
Quelfes	4th & 5th Sunday

Fish Market

Antique Fairs

Lagoa: 2-day event at the Faticil show ground, indoor event 4th Saturday/Sunday (strictly antiques).

Silves: 3rd Saturday (near Continente supermarket); mixed flea market.

Tavira: 1st/5th Saturday.

Vila Real de Santo Antonio: 2nd Saturday in town square or riverfront when other events in square.

Monte Gordo: 4th Saturday. Along the beach front promenade at the rear of the car park.

Vila Real monthly antique market

Fairs Festivals and Exhibitions

The Algarve sees many weekly events throughout the year; in this section we list just some of the major events held annually. To find local events, we suggest checking the local tourist office or local press.

January

Medieval fair held in Paderne: medieval recreation of the middle ages; a five-day event running from the last week in December until beginning of the New Year. With street parades, tournaments, exhibitions of crafts, medieval-style street market, live music.

219

Medieval street beggar in festival spirit

Loulé Chocolate fair (*Festival de Chocolate*): held in the second week of the month, a two-day event normally covering Valentine's day held in the large covered indoor market.

Cycling Tour of the Algarve (Volta ao Algarve) is a major annual event with hundreds of professionals and semi-professionals from across the world. It is held in many different stages; people across the Algarve line the streets cheering them on. Public roads are temporarily closed during the events.

Carnival: Depending when Easter falls the well-known carnival season takes place across the whole of Portugal over a three-day period, with the main carnival procession always taking place on Shrove Tuesday (a public holiday). It is held in most towns and villages across the Algarve.

Monchique Sausage Fair (Feira dos Enchidos Tradicionais de Serra de Monchique): the Monchique Mountain is well known for its self-sufficiency when it comes to produce and is famous for medronho (distilled liquor), honey, and black pork. The fair, held in the first week of March, celebrates local craft with focus on the different types of sausage, with around 50 stalls.

Sausage Festival

International Carnival Sailing Regatta: held in Vilamoura in the first week of March. The first event was held in 1976; it is now attracting up to 300 sailing entrants from around Europe.

Carnivals: see February above.

Faro Flamenco Festival: this colourful festival holds many competitions and workshops for those wanting to take part. First founded in 2004, its success has seen people flock to the event from all across Portugal and Spain. The speed of the tap dancing and spectacular costumes will amaze you! This is held in the second week in March, in the evenings.

April

Tavira Annual Spring fair (Feira da Serra da Primavera de Tavira): this country fair is held over two days, including the public holiday of the 25th (Liberation Day), a large fair with up to 100 stalls. This shows traditional skills of metal work, basket weaving, lace making and traditional food dishes.

Liberation Day: held on the 25th of April; a public holiday that celebrates the fall of the fascist regime in 1974. Many cities and towns hold events and firework displays across the whole of Portugal.

Cake Festival (Folar): held every Easter. The cake is really more like a spicy bread which contains hard boiled eggs complete with the shell and is known in Portugal as Folar. Many towns hold cake festivals. One such place is Guia in central Algarve: it holds a giant cake festival with the cake measuring around two metres in width. Live music and dancing are held in the village centre, at the football ground.

Guia giant cake festival

Flower Festival (Festa das Tochas Floridas): held in Sao Bras de Aportal on Easter Sunday. One of the most spectacular events in the Algarve, with thousands of flowers and petals arranged on the back roads. Men line the streets holding flower-decorated torches and singing 'Hallelujah'.

Open Door: held in Estombar at the winery Quinta Dos Vales, on the first Sunday of the month. Entrance is free; there is live music, dance shows, entertainment. The event offers wine tastings as well as a tour of the wine-making process, many stalls selling traditional crafts and foods. The open day offers the opportunity to wander around the large gardens with unusual art sculptures in the grounds where you will also find many animals in the mini natural zoo. Workshops and free raffle prizes, ideal for a family event. Opening hours 11am – 7pm.

Open door day at Quinta Dos Vales

Albufeira Wine Fair (Bacchus Confraternity): created in 2007 this wine fair gives talks, tastings and tips about the many award-winning wines of Portugal. The fair has around 45-50 wineries who participate, giving a good selection to taste and purchase.

Folk / Wedding Festival: along with many festivals held on May day, celebrated with families heading off to picnic in the many beauty spots the Algarve offers. Alte in central Algarve is just one of many towns that hold a folk festival with traditional music and food. Events will often start on the 31st April.

Pine Cone Festival (Festa da Pinha): held in Estoi in the district of Far, the start of a three-day pilgrimage, celebrated with live bands. Horse parades with decorated carriages; traditional dancing in the evenings; a torch parade with fire. This is a large event well worth visiting.

Sand Sculpture (Feisa): said to be one of the largest sand sculpture exhibitions in Europe, using around 40 tons of sand each year with a different theme, from rock stars to Hollywood. Covering a very large area and open in May until October; entrance fee charged.

Pera yearly Sand sculptures

Corn Festival (Festa da Espiga): a three-day event held in Salir. It may not sound exciting from the title but it is one event not to be missed. A large and celebrated event for the past 40 years, with parades through streets on the first day, and two further days of music and dancing, traditional costumes much on offer with stalls and local food.

Seafood Festival (Festival gastronomia do mar): held in Tavira, Eastern Algarve, over a two-week period. Not a street festival as you would think but held in many participating restaurants, with the focus on celebrating sea food.

Medieval festival: held in the city of Lagos, Western Algarve, a three-day event sometime held towards the end of April. Street processions based on Portugal's Moorish history, with bands, horse displays dressed in period style armour, camels with riders. The festival is just one of the many medieval festival held across the Algarve throughout the year.

June

International Algarve Fair: held in Lagoa in the Fatacul Park along the EN125 in Central Algarve. A two-day event offering many craft stalls, live music and singing on stage, a dog show with competition classes, pony rides, plenty of food stands. Many stalls offer product services, some with free raffle prizes.

Snail Festival (Festival de Caracois): held in Castro Marim near the Spanish border, on the first or second weekend in June. First founded in 2004, the festival offers many ways to cook the snail from Spanish and Portuguese traditional recipes. The festival has grown in size and now attracts many families from Portugal and Spain. There is live music throughout the event.

Folk Festival/Medieval Fair: held in the first week of June in Boliqueime around the village church. With live music and singing, the fair sees locals dress in period costumes. The main theme is traditional local cuisine with open air dining leading into early hours. Free entry.

Film Festival: held in Portimao City in the first week of October, with a wide range of short films including documentaries and animations. Films are submitted each year from across the globe. This is an important event bringing international attention on many subject matters. Free admission.

July

Beer Festival: held in Silves in Central Algarve in the first week of July for 10 days. First celebrated over 35 years ago in the historical city, the event takes place in Fábrica do Inglés with music and singers throughout the 10 days. Many types of beers are served in ceramic mugs which visitors can keep as souvenirs. Traditional food and barbeques are on offer. One for the adults!

Jazz festival (Festival de Jazz): held over three days in the city of Loulé, on the last week of July. First started back in 1995, the festival has grown in popularity and size with jazz players coming from all corners of the planet to partake or just enjoy jam sessions.

Folklore Festival (Festival de Folcore do Azinhal): held in Azinhal just outside Castro Marim. One for all the family, with folk music singing and dancing. Many traditional crafts on show, lacemaking, basket weaving, hat making and costumes. Held in the second or third week in July, continues into the evening.

Seafood Festival (Festa da Ria): the largest held in Faro over a 10-day period running into August; other smaller festivals are also held in other towns and villages. These events are ideal for those who would not order such dishes from a restaurant, not knowing what might turn up at the table. At this event you get to see the many dishes on offer before you buy them, from cataplanas, paellas, mussels, clams and many other delights from the sea. The event starts in the evening with live music and entertainment running the full 10 nights.

Faro Motorbike Rally (Moto Clube Faro): held over a three-day period. One of the largest events of its type in the Algarve, with around 30,000 bikers coming from across the globe. Faro Rally was established in the 1980s. Live music from well-known bands well into early hours. Takes place around the third week of July.

Sweets Art Festival (Feira Concurso Arte Doce): a three-day event held in Lagos at the end of July. This is one for those with a sweet tooth: there are stalls selling all kinds of handmade cakes, chocolate covered figs and many kinds of sweets. The main theme is sculpture, from animals to buildings: all made from marzipan. This attracts a lot of people and is a great family evening event. Opens 6pm – 10pm.

August

Fatacil Showground (Fatacil-Feira de Artisanato, Turismo, Agricultura): the largest and most important fair held in the Algarve. This is one not to be missed. Held over 10 days in the cool evenings of August, it is ideal for families, offering everything all in one place. Artisans come for miles around to show off their skills and wares. There is a spectacular horse arena with events every night; on the other side of the park is music from well-known singers from across Portugal and Europe. Many farm animals are on view, some ideal for petting. Many foods are on offer from all regions: for example, fresh oven-baked breads with cheeses and hams. This is a great entertainment event giving a true taste of Portugal.

10 Day Fatacil Festival evening event

Seafood/shellfish festival (O Festival do Marisco de Olhao): held in Olhao and said to be one of the largest of its kind in the Algarve, established over 25 years ago. A large stage is set up for great evening entertainment of singing and music. For those who love seafood then this festival sees many dishes including paellas. This is an evening outdoor event continuing into the early hours.

Sardine Festivals (Festival de Sardine): these are famous across the Algarve; the largest one is held in Portimao over a 10-day period along the waterfront with evening firework displays. Over six tons of sardines are consumed over the 10 days, with a sardine eating competition: one record was 49 sardines eating in 15 minutes. Others include the Olhos D'Agua sardine festival near Albufeira, a smaller four-day event.

Medieval Festival (Silves Feira Medieval): held in Silves with its castle as the backdrop, making the whole event more believable, this is one of the largest medieval festivals, held over 10 days. It holds re-enactments from the Moorish period: streets fill with jugglers, acrobats and fire breathers, while many stalls from Morocco give the feel of the past. There is an arena with horse jousting. A small fee applies.

Silves annual medieval festival

Seafood Festival (Festa da Ria): held in Fuzeta over a five-day period in the third week in August; first established in 2003. Other smaller festivals are also held in other towns and villages. At this event you get to see the many dishes on offer before you buy them, from cataplanas, paellas, mussels, clams and many other delights from the sea. The event starts in the evenings with music entertainment from different artists every night. It is an ideal family event.

Dried Fruits Fair (Feira Frutos Secos): held in the village of Alcantarilha just off the EN125. A three-day event on the last week in August going into September, celebrating the many different varieties of dried fruits in many forms, from sweets and cakes to preserves and liquors. An early evening event with live music and dancing into the early hours. A good family event offering around 40 stalls and a living museum showing how people lived in the past.

September

Medieval Fair (Salir do Tempo): held in Salir in Eastern Algarve over a three-day period, with fun for all. Locals in period customs really add to the atmosphere. Many stalls with period style banquet; ideal event for families.

Flamenco Festival: held in Lagos over a three-day period in the second week of September. Ideal for those who love to watch this skilful and fast dance, with the unvarying pace of the guitar and costumes that swish and swirl making the whole event mesmerising.

October

Bird Watching Festival: a three-day event that has grown in popularity since its first festival in 2000. It is held in Sagres in Western Algarve and offers field trips and talks on countryside finds; it also offers dolphin watching and horse riding. The area is one of the Algarve's most important areas for wildlife protection: birds which can be observed include storks, eagles, vultures, hawks and falcons. Other areas of importance include salgados (Armacao de Pera) in Central Algarve.

Traditional Fair (Feira de Castro): held on the border of the Algarve and the Alentejo, a two-day event on the third week of October. It has street market stalls selling dried fruits and traditional country produce, including many skilled crafts still used in countryside living. One of the largest fairs of the region, it is well worth the trip inland.

Blip Exhibition (Better Living in Portugal): held in Portimao, Western Algarve, at the Portimao Arena on the first weekend in October. Offering many stands and stalls from services to products, the event is ideal for those looking for information on living in Portugal. It is ideal for browsing more than 100 stall selling crafts, foods, services and Portuguese products and offers staffed care area for children and plenty of space to sit for coffee. Entrance is free.

Blip Exhibition free entrance

Obrigado Festival (Thank you Festival): held in Estombar in Lagoa, a two-day outdoor event held either in September or October. It is themed on cultural exchange, with live music from artists from across Europe, and is set in a protected parkland setting with picturesque views over the lake. It has a children's play area and picnic park, many stalls selling crafts and Portuguese products, and beer and food tents.

November

Sweet Potato fair (Festival da Batata-doce de Aljezur): held in Aljezur in Western Algarve, a three-day event celebrating a gastronomic theme. This is a large event with many craft and food stalls and cooking demonstrations. Enjoy hot sweet jacket potatoes with many different toppings. It is well worth the visit: a good country-style fair with a real taste of the country.

Chestnuts roasted in the street

<u>December</u>

There are just too many events to list at this time of year: nearly every town and city will be holding some kind of Christmas fair, from the large ones in Vila Real St Antonio that lay on an ice skating ring, to the village humble fairs selling handcrafted wear and sweets, cakes and preserves. There are many religious festivals also held this time of year, to the run up to the Feast of the Immaculate Conception. The period ends on Kings Day, or Epiphany, on January 6th.

Charity Santa Swim: held in Armacao de Pera and organized by the Holiday Inn in aid of charity. On Christmas morning at 11am many turn up on the beach in Santa Claus outfits for a charity swim in the ocean. The event has been going over 10 years, come rain or shine; if in the area go down to give your support.

Attractions

Water Parks

Aqua Show

This is one of the largest water parks, offering water roller coaster rides, play pool, water tube slides, wave pool and sea lions and other animal shows. Some rides have age and height restrictions. Open from 1st May until 30th December.

Semino EN396 8125-303 Quarteira Eastern Algarve
Phone: (+351) 289 317 550
www.aquashowparkhotel.com

Aqualand

This water park offers waterslides, include a kamikaze drop waterslide; rapids with inflatable ring rides and hydra pool. There are two children's pools with an adventure castle and play frames. It has a semi-Olympic-size pool for adults and children as well as a surfing wave pool. Open from mid-June until the first week of September.

EN125 – Sítio das Areias Apartado 11 8365-908 Alcantarilha Central Algarve
www.aqualand.pt

Slide & Splash

This is one of the early opening parks, from April to October, offering large water slides, themed rides, water tube slides, a soft slope for younger children. It also puts on reptile and bird of prey shows.

EN125 Vale de Deus-Estombar 8401-901 Lagoa Central Algarve.
Tel: 351 800 202 224
www.slidesplash.com

Theme Parks

Krazy World

Part zoo, part theme park, it also has a crazy golf mini 18-hole course, swimming pool with water slide, children's play area including large bouncy castle, reptile shows with interaction, and tree climbing with zip slides.

Lagoa de Viseu – Estrada Algoz – Messines, 8365-907 Algoz
Tel: 351 282 574 134

Krazy World with mini golf

Zoo Marine

A theme park with much on offer: you can swim with dolphins and sea lions, there are many rides from a Ferris wheel to a small roller coaster, a water park with beach, water slides, tropical bird shows, an aquarium, dolphin shows, pirate-themed action, and – new in 2014 – dinosaur displays.

E N125, Km 65, Guia 8201-864 Albufeira, Central Algarve.
Tel: 351 289 560 300
www.zoomarine.pt

Parque da Mina

A theme park with a difference: the main houses form a museum of how life in the past was lived, while outside are walkways, animals, old horse carts and motor vehicles from different periods. Ideal for families.

Parque da Mina CC1 171 Val de Boi, Caldos de Monchique 855-391
Tel: 351 289 911 622
www.parquedemina.pt

Zoos

Lagos Zoo

Traditional zoo with many kinds of animal, from assorted monkeys, hippos, meerkats, wild cats, birds, reptiles and fish. It also offers a picnic park as well as restaurants.

Quinta Figueiras, Sítio do Medronhal, 8600-013 Barão de São João
Tel: 351 282 680 100
www.lagoszoo.pt

Krazy World (see Theme Parks)

Go Karting

Karting Almancil

This offers Karting for all ages, from electric karts for younger ones to petrol engines for teenagers and adults. It also offers paint ball. Open from February to December.

Kartodromo de Almancil, Caminho das Pereiras, 8135-022 Almancil
Tel: 351 289 399 899

Mini Golf

Family Golf Park

Said to be the largest mini golf park in Europe, this has two 18-hole courses, both on a different theme. The park has restaurants and a children's play area, and also offers rides on a train carriage around Vilamoura.

Rua dos Marmeleiros,Vilamoura,Quarteira, 8125-497, Algarve

Tel: 351 289 300 800
www.familygolfpark.pt

Golf in the Algarve Course information

The first Champion course was built in 1966, designed by the celebrated British golfer Sir Henry Cotton. It was to be a huge challenge turning flat swampland used for crop growing into a respectable golf course to catch serous golfers' attention. With much planting and a good design it proved a huge success. Now in less than 50 years since the first course the Algarve has seen the creation of nearly 40 of some of the best courses in Europe, putting the Algarve into serious contention in many world competitions, including open championships. Below is a brief information guide to help choose the course that may suit your style of playing. Over the years course design has changed not only to make courses challenging, but incorporating what the land and surroundings were used for. In 2008 the Oceânico Nick Faldo & Oceânico O'Connor courses did just that by laying the courses very sympathetically to the surroundings, even incorporating lemon and orange trees, and also with wildlife in mind. Most courses require soft spike shoes.

East Algarve						
Resort	**Holes**	**Length**	**Location**	**Par**	**Construction**	**Required**
Benamor Golf	18	5 ,500 m	Cabanas	69	2000	H/C Cert
Casto Marim	18	5,466 m	Casto Marim	71	2001	H/C Cert
Colina Verde	9	1,145 m	Moncarapacho	28	2003	H/C Cert
Monte Rei Club	18	6,567 m	Vila Real St A	72	2007	H/C Cert
Quinta da Ria	18	6,110 m	Tavira	72	2001	H/C Cert
Quinta de Cima	18	6,256 m	Quinta da Ria	72	1992	H/C Cert
Quinta do Vale	18	6,511	Casto Marim	72	2001	H/C Cert

West Algarve

Resort	Holes	Length	Location	Par	Construction	Required
Álamos Golf	18	5,641 m	Portimao	71	1991	H/C Cert
Alto Golf	18	6,125 m	Alvor	73	1991	H/C Cert
Boavista Golf	18	6,053 m	Lagos	71	2001	H/C Cert
Espiche Golf	18	5,862 m	Lagos	72	U/C	H/C Cert
Oceânico Nick Faldo	18	6,604 m	Silves	72	2008	H/C Cert
Morgado Golf	18	5,399 m	Portimao	73	2003	H/C Cert
Oceânico O'Connor	18	6,719 m	Silves	72	2008	H/C Cert
Palmares Golf	18	5,961 m	Lagos	71	1976	H/C Cert
Parque da Floresta	18	5,670 m	Budens	72	1987	H/C Cert
Penina Championship	18	6,343 m	Alvor	73	1966	H/C Cert
Gramacho	18	5,919 m	Carvoeiro	72	1991	H/C Cert
Vale da Pinta	18	6,152 m	Carvoeiro	72	1992	H/C Cert
Vale de Milho	9	926 m	Carvoeiro	54	1990	N/A

(2 set of tees)

Central Algarve

Resort	Holes	Length	Location	Par	Construction	Required
Balaia Golf Village	9	984m	Abufeira	3	2001	N/A
Oceânico Laguna	18	6,133 m	Vilamoura	73	1990	H/C Cert
Oceânico Millennium	18	6,200 m	Vilamoura	73	2000	H/C Cert
Vilamoura Old Course	18	6,254 m	Vilamoura	72	1969	H/C Cert
Pine Cliffs Golf	2X9	2274 m	Albufeira	67	1991	N/A
Oceânico Pinhal	18	6,300 m	Vilamoura	71	1976	H/C Cert
Pinheiros Altos	18	5,766 m	Almancil	72	1991	H/C Cert
Quinta do Lago (North)	18	6,126 m	Almancil	72	1994	H/C Cert
Quinta do Lago (South)	36	6,488 m	Almancil	74	1994	H/C Cert
Salgados Golf	18	6,080 m	Albufeira	72	1994	H/C Cert

Quick everyday phrases

The Portuguese language is Latin-based so it has a masculine and a feminine with the O being masculine and A being feminine. (Example: 'Thank you' – *Obrigado*, masculine; *Obrigada*, feminine.) The Portuguese phrase is given in bold type, with the pronunciation shown underneath.

Useful Phrases

Good morning   **Bom dia**
bawn deeer

Good afternoon   **Boa traded**
boaer tahrder

Good evening/night   **Boa noite**
boaer noyt

Hello   **Ola**
ollah

Goodbye   **Adeus**
adeeoosh

Please   **Por favour**
poor fe voar

Thank you   **Obrigado(a)**
obreegadoo

Yes/No   **Sim/Nao**
seeng/nahng

Excuse me *(for attention)*   **Desculpe**
dishkoolp

Excuse me *(to pass by)*   **Com licence**
koowm lysaysha

Where is?   **Onde e**
ownder ehh

I'd like   **Queria**
kereer

I don't understand	**Nao Compreendo** nahng comprihendoo
What time is it?	**Que horas sao** ker or say
Do you speak English?	**Fala ingles?** Faler eenglaysh
Open/Closed	**Aberto/Fechado** ahbree/faysher
How much?	**Quanto Custa** kwantoo cushta
Can I have the bill?	**A conta** ahh conta
I would like a beer	**Eu gostaria a cerveja** You goss-ta-reea a sir-veer-ja
I would like a white wine	**Eu gostaria vinho branco** You goss-ta-reea vin-ho branco
I would like a red wine	**Eu gostaria vinho tinto** You goss-ta-reea vin-ho-chin-ko
Bottle of white/red wine	**garrafa de vinho branco/tinto** ga-haffa je vin-ho branco/chin-ko
A cup of tea/coffee	**o cha/o cafe** ta-reea o sha/o caf-aya
I would like a water	**Eu gostaria a agua** You goss-ta-reea a ag-wa
bottle of water	**gaffafa de agua** ga-haffa je ag-wa
Help!	**Socorrer** Socc-or-eh
Where is the hospital?	**Onde e o hospital?** On-dee-ay oo hosh-pee-tal?
Where is the pharmacy?	**Onde e o farmácia?** On-day o farma-see-a?

Where is the dentist?	**Onde e o dentista?**
	On-day o den-teesta?
Where is the police station?	**Onde e o posto da policia?**
	On-day o poss-to da
	pol-its-ia

Other Phrases

Left/Right	**Esquerda/Direita**
Straight ahead	**Sempre em frente**
I'm lost	**Estou doente**
How far?	**Que distancia?**
Today	**Hoje**
Tomorrow	**Amanha**
Yesterday	**Ontem**
Weekend	**Fim-de-semana**
How much?	**Quanto**
Big/Small	**Grande/Pequeno**
Too much	**Demasiado**
What is that?	**Quanto e?**
Is it free of charge?	**Esta livre?**
Can I have?	**Pode dar-me**
Hot/Cold	**Frio/Quente**
Not working	**Nao Funciona**
I'd like the toilet	**Queria Casa-de-banho**
Where can I find?	**Onde posso encontrar?**
I'd like more please	**Queria mais Por favour**
Do you have?	**Tem?**
No more thank you	**Nao mais Obrigado/a**
Petrol/Diesel	**Gasolina/gasoleo**

Pre payment	**Pre pagamento**
Self Service	**Eu Servico**

Index

D

E

F

Z

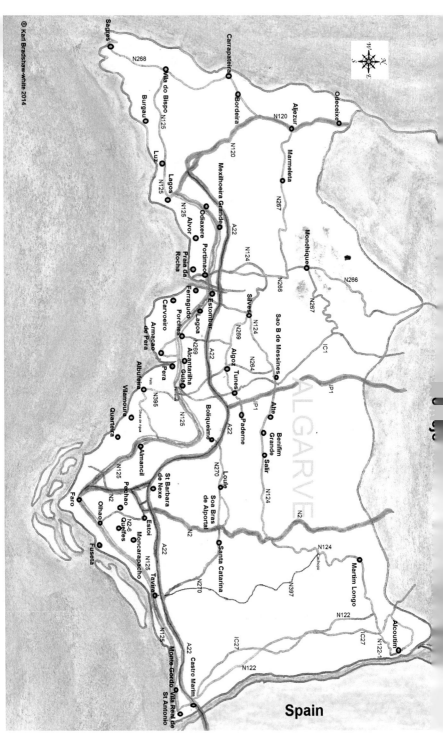

Spain